ADVENTURES
in
MANAGEMENT

ADVENTURES
in
MANAGEMENT

ADVENTURES
in
MANAGEMENT

A Saga of Managing
in a Developing Country

Kenneth Abeywickrama

Response Books
A division of Sage Publications
New Delhi/Thousand Oaks/London

First published in 2007 by

Response Books
A division of Sage Publications India Pvt Ltd
B-42, Panchsheel Enclave
New Delhi – 110 017

Sage Publications Inc
2455 Teller Road
Thousand Oaks, California 91320

Sage Publications Ltd
1 Oliver's Yard, 55 City Road
London EC1Y 1SP

Published by Tejeshwar Singh for Response Books, phototypeset in 11.5/13 pts ACaslon Regular by Star Compugraphics Private Limited, Delhi and printed at Chaman Enterprises, New Delhi.

Library of Congress Cataloging-in-Publication Data Available

ISBN: 10: 0-7619-3550-9 (PB)   10: 81-7829-709-4 (India-PB)
          13: 978-0-7619-3550-6 (PB) 13: 978-81-7829-709-5 (India-PB)

Production Team: Kuhu Tanvir, Anupama Purohit, Mathew, P.J. and Santosh Rawat

To my wife,
Bernadette,
who urged me to write
about my life experiences.

CONTENTS

PREFACE

'WHAT MAKES A GOOD MANAGER?' IS AN ISSUE THAT WILL BE ARGUED over for eternity. In a world increasingly influenced by the board-rooms of transnational corporations that guide the global economy and much of its political policies, this question is more important today than the traditionally inconclusive blockbusters like 'Is there a living God?' or 'What is the origin of the universe?'. Managers make things happen. They re-shape the universe we live in, perhaps more so than the world's political leaders. Choosing top managers is as important as choosing politicians who govern us, whether it is in a developed or a developing country. Yet many developing countries, much more than developed countries, seem to fail in making the right choices.

This book contains some of my rewarding, and unrewarding, personal adventures that I believe helped to shape whatever man-agement abilities I had while working in Sri Lanka that gained recognition in some international circles at one time. It begins with my formative years as a junior manager in the state-owned port corporation, followed by 14 years as a senior manager in a subsidiary of a large multinational corporation, to a period of nearly three years as the Chairman/Managing Director of a large state-owned enterprise. Later, as an international consultant, I tried to introduce some of these management lessons to companies and government officials in Africa, East Europe and South Asia, with varying de-grees of success.

Some aspects of my work in the State Timber Corporation were dealt with in a case study at the Harvard Business School (State

Timber Corporation of Sri Lanka, Ref. 9-382-019) and in an article in the *California Management Review* (Vol. XXVIII, No. 3, Spring 1986). However, for obvious reasons of expediency, some of the internal workings of the business could not be revealed by those of us in the business at the time. Those restraints do not hold today and the story can be told in more detail.

Most studies of managerial behaviour are from the perspectives of the developed countries, where most transnational corporations are located in and from where the levers of the world economy are handled. But developing countries are increasingly becoming a part of the global economy. Are successful managers in developing countries the same as those in developed countries? Not entirely. The politics of developing countries, the social structures, the cultural attitudes of people, are often dissimilar and cannot be carbon copies of their counterparts in developed countries. Even multinational corporations, which have developed very successful systems of management, perform somewhat differently in many developing countries because of the cultural attitudes that influence local managers and other employees. But this is not the only rationale for this very personal story. Those of us who have worked in many different countries realize, after a while, that there are more similarities than dissimilarities among people throughout the world.

An issue for management in developing countries is the pervasive role of politicians and their corrupt cronies. Corruption is not a Third World phenomenon. Big money corrupts and there is ample evidence of political patronage of business in all developed industrialized countries. But corruption here, in the industrialized world, is considered an evil and, though it cannot be eliminated, there are some legal controls and some degree of public outrage when the media exposes scandals. But in many developing countries, legal restraints are diluted and civil society is apathetic, taking for granted that politicians will be corrupt and that the only recourse for ordinary citizens is to work within the system. Top managers have to work within this system on the basis of each individual's personal philosophy and morals.

The human frailties of powerful political and business leaders is a subject that is much like sex education for children. It is a subject that is broached with great caution. Management writers would rather avoid this subject. Local citizens would not care to dwell on it for fear of harassment. So much of it passes unnoticed for want of a vigilant citizenry and the paucity of investigative media reporting. Yet it is a core issue which will determine a country's progress. This is a subject that will crop up throughout this book, illustrated by real life experiences, unlike the theories and impersonal stories in many management textbooks.

Managing people and making them productive is not achieved by a mastery of management techniques learnt in classrooms alone. Academic learning is a foundation, but top managers develop their own philosophy of management over time through background experiences in real life situations. It evolves over time, if they care to learn. It will be shaped by personal morality. I believe that my own philosophy of management evolved over this period by being sensitive to the needs of the market or consumers and the aspirations and concerns of the people I had to work within these organizations. On the balance, I believe I was influenced in my development more by my subordinates than my superiors. But it was a long drawn out process and I was hardly conscious of the changes in myself till much later times, when I had the leisure to reflect on my own work.

The core lesson I have learnt, and which I try to illustrate throughout, is that ordinary human beings in developing countries are endowed with a high degree of intelligence, capacity for hard work, loyalty and innate decency. The worker or ordinary employee is rarely given much credit for the success of a business. In developing countries, the kudos is often reserved for the political bosses, not even for the top operating managers. But good management is the key to the development of the developing world, much more so than foreign investment or foreign aid. Without it, the talents of the people and the resources of the countries are wasted.

The good news is that the backward cultural baggage of a wider society (and which society does not have some form of it?) need not hinder a business. It is within the capacity of the top management to create its own harmonious culture within the business and create an environment that works for the advantage of the business and the benefit and dignity of the employees. Many readers may disagree with some of the tactics I used in overcoming management and political obstacles as described here. But management, like politics, is the art of the possible.

ACKNOWLEDGEMENTS

To Stephen Keiley,
Marcia Wiss,
Victor Santhiapillai,
Professor Stanley Samarasinghe,
Olcott Gunasekera
and my other friends
who encouraged me
to publish my writing.

I

MANAGING amid CHAOS

For Forms of Government let fools contest;
Whate'er is best administered is best:
For Modes of Faith let graceless zealots fight;
He can't be wrong whose life is in the right:
In Faith and Hope the world will disagree,
But all Mankind's concern is Charity:
All must be false that thwart this One great End,
And all of God, that bless Mankind or mend.

—Alexander Pope, *An Essay on Man,*
Epistle III, circa A.D. 1744

1

MANAGING amid CHAOS

COPING WITH CHAOS

THE PORTS OF SRI LANKA (THEN OFFICIALLY CALLED CEYLON) WERE nationalized in 1958 and the top management team that took charge comprised distinguished Civil Servants. The Ceylon Civil Service at the time had a different connotation derived from the traditions of the British colonial service. These were people who had, after graduation from the University of Ceylon (the one and only university in the country, which was also allied at the time with the University of London for academic standards), had topped the national list in a competitive exam to be selected as a special grade of public service mandarins. Though entrants had to be younger than 24 years of age, they were destined for the top management in public service from their earliest years. The band of men who took the top management of the Port Cargo Corporation were in their early forties and were already senior public servants who had headed large government departments and were attracted to service in the newly created government corporate sector with its higher salaries and perquisites that were offered as inducements. But the Port Cargo Corporation, with its labour unions and the wily remnants of the private sector wharf company staff who still remained in service, often managed to confound these honourable men of obvious intellect.

The 1956 'Peoples' Revolution' in Sri Lanka of left-wing, nationalist and communalist elements that gained parliamentary power had ushered in a period of political and social chaos, mostly unintended, since the movement contained both men of goodwill as well as political adventurers. While it provided an outlet for the frustrations of large sections of ordinary people whose voices were lost in the politics dominated by the small wealthy urban upper-class, it also showed that emotion alone does not provide a basis for a good government. The nationalization of the ports and the transport services, among other acquisitions of private business, had an adverse impact on services to the public and on economic activity.

The ports had, in total, about 40,000 employees and the bus transport companies had a similar number. These work places became the battlegrounds for warring left-wing trade unions, each vying for control over the majority of the workers. The trade unions were backed by leaders of political parties who were now cabinet ministers, prepared to interfere in management operations in a way that had never been seen before in the country and would be considered illegal in most democracies. Workers were the weapons used in the battles for political advantage, they were not seen as people whose interests should have been a matter of primary concern for their leaders.

Union leaders tried to prove to the workers that their unions alone could obtain more petty concessions and intimidate managements. Work stoppages were commonplace, the pace of work often came close to organized idleness and the output of work diminished to the extent that it took a heavy toll on the economy of the country. The delays in handling cargo in the Port of Colombo, the main national port, led to long lines of waiting ships outside the harbour, increased demurrage charges by foreign ship owners and increased costs to exporters and importers. It was a deterrent to any new large-scale private investment in the country.

The private stevedoring companies, prior to nationalization, had been managed by expatriate managers, supported by subordinate local managers, most of whom did not have higher education. After nationalization, the expatriates left the country or joined other foreign-owned mercantile establishments, leaving only the local staff that could not find employment elsewhere. The ex-Civil Servants who were now at the helm saw this as a major handicap and speedily recruited a batch of a dozen management trainees with a university education background in order to create the next line of top managers. That is how I came to be recruited to the Port Cargo Corporation, together with 12 others from the University of Ceylon of my era. We, in turn, were attracted to the corporation by salaries that were much higher than in the equivalent public service positions.

This recruitment set the stage for what is a familiar situation in many organizations, military and civilian, where older long serving employees with lesser qualifications find that much younger people are being groomed to be their superiors. The top management of senior civil servants, knowing little of port operations or, more importantly, how to organize such a vast unruly labour force, were perplexed and confounded by the introduction of politics into corporate governance. They confined themselves to their rooms in the upper floors of the port offices, removed from the chaos of the wharves and surrounded by the loyal clerks and secretaries they had brought with them from the public services. The middle management, left over from the private stevedoring companies, ran the stevedoring and wharf operations. The new management trainees were schooled by them in the existing port practices (they hardly merit the name of management systems) to enable them to continue the primitive operations that were costing the country so dearly.

As newcomers to the Port of Colombo in 1959, it took us awhile to get accustomed to the teeming crowds and confusion in the port. The infrastructure of the port had been developed since the country gained independence in 1948 with assistance from the UK and it had acquired three new quays for berthing large ships. At the time, the port could accommodate 32 to 36 ships, depending on size. But by 1959, through neglect and indifferent management, the buildings and offices were becoming grimy and the warehouses and yards were a scene of confusion. Wharf clerks, employed by clearing houses and large importers, often showed great skill in locating their cargo amidst this confusion. Port workers, workers employed by transport agents and others not easily identified, walked around or sat in shady corners smoking *beedis*[1] or chewing betel[2] and spitting blood red betel juice. The place was infested with rats and cockroaches. Managers who occupied the Operations Room at night (all super-intendents were on a roster for work supervision during the night shift) would literally see hundreds of cockroaches emerging from nooks and crannies to swarm around the office and critically watch the managers at work.

How do managers cope, as people of integrity and goodwill, in this miasma caused by the political bosses who run the country? My first supervisor, the Wharf Manager of the ports in 1960, a senior civil servant who had held high positions in the public admin-istration and a man of high intelligence, integrity and decency, offered one model. It allowed the Wharf Department to seemingly operate with a purpose, to maintain the form that there was order and discipline around his office, without in any way improving the port services to the customers, mainly large import or export com-panies and the general public the port was intended to serve. In a no-win situation it was perhaps better to escape reality to preserve sanity and self-respect.

The chaos in the port resulted in frequent damage to cargo and the loss of goods in handling. These problems were connected with employee indiscipline and thieving and could not be addressed without a showdown with the unions which the top management could not contemplate. The only solution was to allow the insurance companies to compensate the customers for their losses without the management losing face, of course, at an increasing cost to business and the national economy. To pass an insurance claim, the

[1] *Beedis* are little cigarettes with tobacco pieces wrapped in a leaf. It was the favourite smoke of the poor as it was cheap and strong.

[2] The chewing leaf commonly used by people throughout South Asia for relaxation.

customer had to get a letter from the port disclaiming liability for loss or damage, once the carrier vessel proved that it had delivered the cargo in 'good order' as certified in the 'boat notes.' The Wharf Manager called up his two Staff Assistants, of whom I was one, and drafted for us 32 standard letters of disclaimer where the port authorities declined responsibility for loss or damage, under varied pretexts, in all instances.

These 32 letters, numbered individually, were given to both of us and the Chief Clerk who supervised over a group of 30 odd clerks, stenographers, typists and peons. We received about 50 letters of complaint daily from consignees. These letters were first opened by the Chief Clerk who then had these recorded in a register and called for the relevant file from one of his clerks. After checking the file, and making any observations of his own, he forwarded them to one of the Staff Assistants, meaning the two of us, with the minute '*Mr. A. - For your action, pl.*'

The letters would be carried to our desks by a peon, one of those indispensable odd bodies who formed the lowest rank in the office hierarchy, serving tea, running errands for the bosses but also acting as guardians of the office by denying the ordinary public easy access to the office unless they were suitably appreciated or rewarded. We would examine the letter of complaint and decide on an appropriate standard answer and note the number on the margin within a circle and initial it. These went back to the Chief Clerk who then passed these on to the typists who also had the indicative numbers for the standard letters. When these were typed and returned, the Chief Clerk checked the letters for accuracy and initialled the office copy to certify that they were in order. The letters came back to us for signature. After our signature, the letters went to a filing clerk who put them in addressed envelopes and filed the office copies of the letters. Before despatch for posting, the date of despatch was entered in a register for record purposes. All of this was seemingly efficient and business-like.

If a company that was a customer, or an insurance company had the temerity to challenge our disclaimer and produce evidence to prove that there had been wilful negligence by the port authorities, the final bombshell awaited the complainant. We would send the ultimate disclaimer: 'We accept no liability for losses or damages sustained in the Queen's Warehouse'.[3] By the inherited English law, the government not be sued nor could the port warehouses belonging to the Port Commission which was also a government department.

In the rarefied air of the Port head offices, the semblance of order and servility that characterized the old public service continued. No subordinate dared to invade the office of the Wharf Manager, while the Chief Clerk was like a school headmaster and was addressed as 'Sir' by his staff and treated with deference. Every morning, the Chief Clerk arrived early and at, 8.30 a.m., drew a red line on the attendance register which all the minor staff, as opposed to us, executives, had to sign on arrival. Since the register was then placed on the Wharf Manager's desk, any subordinate arriving late preferred to apply for a day's leave from the Chief Clerk rather than enter the haloed sanctuary of the boss and confront his stern gaze.

But out in the wharves, where the real action took place, the picture was grim. The top managers rarely ventured out into this dangerous zone, except on special occasions. Once when the Wharf Manager did venture out on one of these occasions to check on the physical condition of a warehouse, a hilarious situation arose.

To understand what took place, it will be necessary to acquaint the reader with the cargo handling practices of a bygone era. Most cargo came in bags or boxes and these were manually loaded onto rope slings, in the form of nets or plain circular ropes. This cargo was stacked onto the slings by stevedores working in the ship's hold, lifted onto to the quay by the ship's winches and unloaded by shore labour that moved these into a warehouse using handcarts.[4] When

[3] The Queen of the United Kingdom was at the time the titular head of state of Ceylon, as it was then known.

[4] Heavier cargo was lifted by big shore cranes and the largest by giant floating cranes.

the slings were landed, two tally clerks, one working for the shipping agent and the other for the port corporation, tallied the cargo at each unloading point to keep a count of the cargo by consignees' marks and numbers and quantities, to safeguard the interests of their respective organizations. While agent's tally clerks, being employees of private companies, were conscientious about their work, the port corporation tally clerks usually took time off and later copied the tally sheets of the agent's clerks.

On this day, when the Wharf Manager was walking along Queen Elizabeth Quay where four cargo vessels were being unloaded, he passed a port corporation tally clerk who was resting in the shade of a warehouse smoking a cigarette. I was accompanying my manager so, perhaps, he needed to maintain his profile as the boss. He walked up to the tally clerk and sternly reprimanded him, 'Get on with your work. You should be working instead of resting.' The tally clerk gave him a contemptuous look and asked him to mind his own business. This was too much to stomach. The Wharf Manager walked to the office of the Quay Superintendent and directed him to interdict the clerk from work with immediate effect and then went back to his office. The offending clerk was summoned by the superintendent and told to hand over his documents, was handed a letter of interdiction, and asked to leave the premises. The poor man was distraught and contrite. 'What did I do, Sir?' he begged. 'You fool, you insulted our big boss. Don't you know the Wharf Manager?' 'How do I know he is the Wharf Manager? I have never seen him. I thought he was a cheeky consignee. Please save me, Sir'. 'Well, now you know' was the discomfiting response he got.

The matter was settled shortly afterwards. Nobody at management level wanted any union involvement in the matter. The clerk submitted a humble apology, which was accepted, and he resumed work, with the loss of half day's pay for the time he was under interdiction.

Face saving is a feature of management in more organizations than management educators would like to admit. In fact, techniques of face saving should be a compulsory subject in management education though, I must confess, I have never yet encountered the subject in any management study. But I have seen many leaders, in the business sector, in the army and in politics, holding their heads high and walking with aplomb without ever acknowledging that they had limited control over their organizations for better or worse. Those who are less talented in this art perhaps constitute the wrecks of management or the ranks of the unemployed.

2

PROLETARIAN POWER

'SIR, THIS IS THE SUPERINTENDENT OF BAGHDAD QUAY REPORTING. All six gangs of stevedores on the *ss*. Hokkaido Maru have stopped work for the last two hours and refuse to start work unless we order fresh dinner. They claim the fish in their dinner is spoilt.' I phoned the Operations Manager in the Control Room and sought his guidance.

'You know very well they are lying. Tell them to start work right away,' was the curt order I received.

The scene was the Port of Colombo in 1961. I was a rookie Junior Staff Officer in the then Port Cargo Corporation, formed out of the nationalization of the private stevedoring companies in 1958 by the then 'socialist government' that stormed into power in 1956. The Port of Colombo, the main national port, had become a battleground for the trade unions allied to the three left-wing parties in the government seeking the loyalty of a majority of the forty thousand odd workers in the ports. Trade union leaders like Pantis and Alexander wielded more power than the top management as they had direct access to senior cabinet ministers, while managers walked the tricky tight rope between the demands of managing a business and the threat of punishment at the hands of the labour unions or their political bosses.

In this surreal world, each work gang on board a ship had four winchmen[1] where two were needed and 14 stevedores worked in a

[1] The men who operated the ship's winches, the standard for unloading cargo before the era of container ships.

ship's hold where six men would have more than sufficed. When on board, by common consent, stevedores sub-divided their gangs of 12 into gangs of three or four persons so that each mini gang worked only for three or four hours. These unofficial work shifts were called *pori* in port parlance and was wisely ignored by labour supervisors who valued their own health. An output of 40 tons of cargo per gang per shift was considered a good norm where an average of 200 tons was possible. When ship owners needed a better cargo output, the local shipping agent's representative would negotiate with the gang foremen and pay a special gratuity that exceeded the workers' daily wage for a fixed tonnage of output from a ship. Port officers turned a blind eye to these established practices and pretended they did not exist.

Stevedores had ways of extorting payments from contractors working in the port. Workers received free meals on board while at work as a bonus given by the port management. The basic menu was fixed by the Personnel Division of the port which negotiated the meal contracts with caterers. The lunch and dinner packets given to port workers were considered so good that they were sold on the streets outside the port entrances by street hawkers for premium prices with cries of *varaye buth* or 'harbour meals', a connotation that had achieved the status of a good brand name. The meals were sold not because these were not appreciated by the workers, it was simply that some workers needed urgent cash for a *ganja* (marijuana) smoke more than a meal.

Periodically, powerful groups of workers would extract payments from the meal contractors as the price of doing business in the port. If the contractor would not oblige, they would stage a work stoppage claiming the meal was spoilt and demand fresh meals as replacements. Some special methods would reinforce their claim. Boiled cockroaches or worms would be brought and mixed in a meal packet to prove their point to the investigating labour supervisor or superintendent. No one was fooled by the hoax but neither was anyone willing to risk a confrontation with the labour. But a rookie junior staff officer had still to learn the ways of the world.

Afraid of displeasing the Operations Manager and losing his respect, I boarded a launch and went to the ship anchored in midstream. The Labour Supervisor responsible for work on the ship and an Assistant Superintendent reluctantly came aboard the launch to accompany me. I boarded the ship, climbing a long gangway, and was immediately surrounded by scores of riotous workers on board loudly demanding new food parcels. Taking a dinner parcel, I tasted a mouthful, pronounced it good, and sharply ordered the men to start work. There was a rising chorus of discontent from the men around me while those unseen in the background could be heard saying, 'He has eaten a good dinner at the Taprobane Hotel and wants us to eat rotten meals' and 'Throw him overboard.'

Surrounded by a rowdy mob of ill-kempt stevedores, each carrying a nasty looking steel cargo hook, the tool of trade of stevedores of that era, I was quite intimidated. I looked around and saw that the Assistant Superintendent, Labour Supervisor and the boat crew had already deserted the ship and boarded the launch that was started up. Mustering as much dignity as I could and muttering that I would see what I could do, I retreated to the gangway and thankfully made it to the launch, unmolested.

Coming ashore and entering the dinghy little office in the wharf, the Assistant Superintendent indulgently smiled and said, 'Sir, just let me call the meal contractor and ask for a supply of fresh meals. You just note in the Log Book that the meals were spoilt.' All was well afterwards and the subject was closed.

My experiences in this area were dwarfed by the experiences of some of the other rookie junior managers in the port. Lambert was a conscientious young wharf superintendent who headed the large Prince Vijaya Quay, with a workforce of around 3,000, working as stevedores, warehouse labourers, checkers, clerks, supervisors, among others. The quay was an important site as it handled most of the bulk food grains that were imported into the country. One of the leading left-wing trade unions decided to cut the enthusiastic young officer to size.

The hectic morning activity in the wharves was the mustering of the labour to be allocated to the ships' holds that were to be worked. This painstaking task[2] took at least an hour and a half and cut into the time available for actual work. Quay superintendents had to arrive at 6.30 a.m. to ensure that the 7.00 a.m. muster would commence on time. Many labour supervisors, being poorly educated political appointees promoted from the ranks of labour, had great difficulty reading the muster rolls, causing more delays. In this instance, one labour union started the practice of holding a public political meeting lasting half an hour at the time the muster commenced. This held up work for half an hour. The Superintendent, Lambert, spoke to the union leader, Pantis, and asked him to hold the meetings after the work shift ended. Pantis responded: 'You do your job, Sir, I will do mine.'

Feeling helpless, Lambert dutifully sought guidance from the Captain, the Chief Operations Manager, a burly and seemingly tough ex-sea captain who had also been the former Master Attendant (Harbour Master) of the Port of Colombo. 'Give him a written warning,' growled the Chief. Lambert issued Pantis a warning which the recipient publicly threw away. Lambert again sought the guidance of the Chief. 'Issue him a charge sheet,' he was advised. This was duly done but it still had no effect. But it did have repercussion. Lambert's wife received anonymous phone calls advising her to watch out for her husband as he could suffer an unforeseen accident while travelling to work on his motorcycle. This put so much pressure on the poor fellow that he reported sick and stayed away from work. By now, the union leadership had assessed that Lambert had been brought to heel and the morning political meetings ceased. Lambert returned to work a chastened man. No action was ever taken against the union leaders. Nor did any among the senior management visit the contentious site to make inquiries or show support for their junior.

[2] The archaic system of mustering labour for work in Sri Lankan workplaces will be dealt with in a later section on work systems.

Powerful managers can sometimes be like some strong military commanders. They issue stern orders to the subordinates manning the frontlines and vow that there will be no retreat from hostile territory. But they shun the frontlines of the war zone themselves, and turn a blind eye to the human losses suffered in the struggle. The trade union leaders knew that the management would be too timid to enforce discipline and that the young manager was used as a tool to save face. Sadly, we young managers were not yet men of the world at the time. I had learnt two valuable lessons in management politics: one, senior managers who appear to have control over situations may have very little, and two, that bosses tend to seek a gullible junior as a scapegoat when confronted with awkward situations. It was a case of 'I save face' even though you lose face, because you are the smaller guy.

But the most important lesson, that discipline must be enforced, even with some brutality at times, eluded me at the time and sank into my consciousness only much later. For unfortunately, the appearance of timidity seems to bring out the bullying instinct in most undisciplined groups of men, and sometimes, even in good men. The following story is an example of this phenomenon.

Stevedores in the port looked unkempt and disorderly to most European eyes. They dressed poorly in nondescript attire, spoke loudly, lazed around and tended to wander around the ships with an eye for thieving. European ships crews treated them with disdain and spoke to them roughly. Officers treated foremen and supervisors who came for orders or requests condescendingly. The stevedores understood this and kept their distance from these people.

A number of Chinese ships from mainland China were regular visitors to the port in the 1960s as the country was importing a lot of rice from China on a barter agreement in exchange for rubber. This began with the international trade embargo led by the USA against the communist government in that country. Ceylon ignored this embargo in its own interests of national food security. Chinese crew members were generally people of short stature, like many Sri Lankans, and were reserved in manner and polite to the local workers. This tended to be mistaken for weakness or timidity. During the unloading operations on one Chinese cargo ship, berthed in mid-stream, the theft of clothes and other articles left unattended had taken alarming proportions. The ship's officers then came out to address the 120 odd stevedores working on the ship, to register their protest and demand an end to these activities. The stevedores retaliated by threatening the officers and driving them away back to their cabins.

There was a short period of quiet on board after this. The stevedores went back to their work while the ship's crew gathered in their dining room for an emergency meeting. One could imagine them saying, 'Comrades, how do we deal with these proletarians who do not show any respect for our great country?' or 'How does the Great Helmsman, Comrade Mao, advice us to act in such situations?' Whatever it is that they discussed, the Chinese had not only read the little Red Book but had also practiced their martial arts. The 25 crew members came out of the meeting with raucous shouts and menacing looks on their faces and attacked the stevedores who outnumbered them five times over. The attack was so concentrated and violent and the martial cries so frightening that our stevedores were soon screaming *Buddhu Ammo*[3] in terror and jumping into the sea and swimming ashore.

They arrived in total disarray at their superintendent's office and refused to work on the ship, claiming assault without cause by the crew. The superintendent asked for help from higher managers but the stevedores were adamant that they would not work on this ship and this was later endorsed by the workers' unions. The matter then went up to the level of the ministry in charge of ports and, finally, the cabinet minister in charge informed the Chinese embassy. The Chinese Ambassador, who wished to end the stand off, then came to the port and apologised to the workers' unions and assured them that these incidents would not be repeated. This settled the

[3] 'Holy Mother' would be a rough translation. This is a common cry of distress in the colloquial Sinhala language.

problem. It also ensured that hereafter the Chinese crews were treated with a lot more respect.

The Japanese management practice of innovation and development through genuine employee participation and suggestions was not known in the nineteen sixties in Sri Lanka, in fact it is still unknown today to most of the business world, even in advanced industrial countries. A good employee is one who closes his mind, follows orders and carries out the existing work practices. Changes can be made by top management but altering existing practices is the most difficult task. Resistance to real change, meaning changes to the core management practices, is almost a universal human failing, except in the most dynamic of corporate cultures. In a developing country like Sri Lanka, where research is a rarity and inquiring minds tend to be stifled from their school going and university days through learning by rote and the force of traditional authority, changes in business practices are indeed uncommon.

The Port of Colombo and the other minor ports of Galle, Trincomalee and Point Pedro seemed locked in the 1800s. Around 1835, when the Port of Colombo was being developed by British colonial rulers to serve the commercial interests of the expanding tea plantations and the growing import/export business, the port authorities brought in labour, supervisors and the port management practices of Bombay in India. This was a modern system to the Ceylon of that age. The Marathi labourers from India were illiterate and the number of these casual labourers available for any work shift could not be estimated in advance. The systems were designed for these conditions.

By the beginning of the 20th century, local workers had replaced the Marathis. The old systems continued. To the European managers and their Ceylonese subordinates, the workers were 'coolies' who were identified by numbers, needing verbal orders to work. Even in the 1960s, though conditions had changed with more mechanization, a permanent cadre of port workers, and more literate employees, this very primitive system of operations continued.

Labour was 'mustered' every morning,[4] a practice that continues in tea plantations even today in deference to colonial tradition. By 6.30 a.m. in the morning and 4.30 p.m. in the evening, wharf superintendents instructed labour supervisors at each stevedoring unit about the allocation of work gangs for the next shift, both on board ships by cargo hatches and alongside warehouses by unloading points. Half an hour later the muster supervisors took up positions at different mustering points and shouted out the workers' identification numbers. Workers were called according to their 'token numbers', such as 'A128', 'B360', etc. As a number was called, the worker identified would come up and surrender his tin token with his number, a round metal disc with a stamped number and a hole in the centre of the disc. When the requisite number required for a work gang was obtained,[5] these tokens would be put into a wire carrier (hence the need for the hole in the disc) and given to a gang foreman, called a *tindal*, with instructions about the ship and the hatch his gang had to work in.

This task, carried out at 7.00 a.m. in the morning and again at 5.00 p.m. in the evening throughout the port area, involving about 15,000 jostling and shouting men in each work-shift, created a scene of medieval chaos. When a shift was over, the gang foremen returned these tokens to the supervisors and these went again to the pay clerks to write up the pay registers. Naturally, about two to three hours of work time was lost during each shift on account of 'mustering'.

Workers in the port were not very proficient or even very interested in their work because they had no professional job training. New arrivals went on the job, observed others and learnt both good and bad practices. Handling the ship's winches requires more skill than manually hauling bagged cargo with steel cargo hooks (the basic tool of the old stevedore) into a sling. A winchman enjoyed a higher grade and pay than an ordinary stevedore. But there was

[4] The practice also existed in the tea plantations.

[5] 12 hatch labourers, four winchmen and a gang foreman for a ship's work gang.

no formal training for this work. Ambitious workers bribed the winchmen to allow them to handle the winches, a practice that was forbidden, because it was the only way they could learn, even if they sometimes caused damage to cargo through incorrect handling of the winches.

It did not occur to anyone at the top management level to strive to change these systems, though many went on familiarization visits to modern ports around the world. After all, in a poor country, foreign trips to affluent nations are regarded more as paid holidays than work assignments. In modern ports stevedores are attached to fixed work teams. The work teams read the work allocations on notice boards and get to their work points and commence work without much ado. But no one in the Port Corporation of Ceylon wanted to buck the system. It was too dangerous to expose oneself as a critic of the existing system that had been hallowed by over a hundred years of practice. The top management did not review performances against targets or evaluate costs according to reasonable norms. The routine work procedures were more important than the results.

In fairness to the Captain, the Chief Operations Manager, it must be said that he sometimes talked of the need to set up a stevedores' training school in the port. But nothing ever came of the idea. It was probably reckoned too costly and wasteful by those higher up in the hierarchy.

A few years later, I was recruited as a Senior Marketing Manager in a multinational corporation that was the biggest consumer products marketing company in the country. Being eager to learn about modern marketing management, I asked my supervisor, the director in charge, advice on what management books I should read on my speciality. His answer was revealing: 'Don't bother to read books. Just follow my instructions and do what we are already doing in this office.' Fortunately, multinational corporations have good management systems but by now I was sceptical about advice from superiors and therefore profitably spent time, for the rest of my working career in that company, reading practically every book by written by Peter Drucker, who then became my management guru.

3

LEARNING FROM SUBORDINATES

TO ACCEPT THAT ORDINARY WORKERS, WHO ARE OFTEN REGARDED as a somewhat cruder and intellectually inferior species of humanity, are mostly decent and intelligent people who can perform at high levels of competence, given the right circumstances and training, is not easy in a developing country environment. It requires a suspension of prevailing middle class cultural values about subordinate classes that are imbued by managers from the upper social class since childhood. It was a lesson that I learnt early in my working life. It was not easy to comprehend this reality at first while working in the Port of Colombo.

As young stevedoring superintendents, standing early morning at the first floor windows of the old Admiralty Building in the port, we watched with unease and trepidation as thousands of harbour workers streamed in for work through the Kochchikade Gate. They came from the wretched slums in the northern side of Colombo, with names like Grandpass, Kochchikaday, Maha Modera, Wellampitiya and Mariakadday. They had the distinct aspect of a dangerous and unruly mob. Dressed in shirts and sarongs that were often raised for convenience of movement high enough to reveal underpants, or the lack of them, they shouted greetings to each other using the grossest obscenities concerning each others mothers and their recent sleeping habits. At least half their working time was spent in idleness at work points; sleeping, gambling or smoking marijuana.

By common consent, any work gang of twelve men re-divided themselves into three shifts of four men each, giving each man plenty of rest time. Thieving was rampant. Ship's crews would complain that sailors' underwear, often washed and hung up to dry near port-holes, were robbed by stevedores. Underwear could be easily pilfered as the thief had only to wear it under his sarong and evade detection. If liquor was unloaded, the winchmen ensured that a case crashed on the pier while men waiting with buckets collected the golden liquid that poured out of the case.

While the port management failed to discipline these men in these matters, the labour unions enforced discipline on their members and ensured that there were no fights, gang wars among workers or disobedience of union orders. The union leaders had the means that the management lacked.

A few years after I started work as a Wharf Superintendent, the Captain, the Chief Operations Manager of the ports, summoned me. This gruff and burly ex-merchant navy captain, famed for his vulgar slang and bullying manner while dealing with his staff, was at heart a decent man in an old fashioned way. He said that the port was losing millions of rupees each year because the gear used in cargo handling was often damaged or lost and therefore not delivered on time. (I was not privy to the record, but almost certainly the issue had been raised by the external auditors and discussed at a board meeting). The gear consisted of thousands of rope and net slings, wire slings, cable slings and more sophisticated handling equipment like cranes. The large shore cranes on the quays and floating cranes in the water were owned by the Port Commission, then a government department, and were hired daily by the port corporation as per requirement. He said he was creating a new operations unit called the Cargo Gear Unit of which I was to be the superintendent. There was already an Assistant Superintendent in charge of this work but he lacked competence and hence the problems.

I responded frankly that I knew nothing of stores management. He said I could learn a lot by visiting the stores department of the Government Factory at Kolonnawa, the premier government work-shop in the country at the time, and that he would arrange with the General Manager of the Government Factory for me to be a visitor for about a week.[1] Satisfied, I returned to the Admiralty Office and told my Stevedoring Manager, a kindly man who often treated me like a well meaning uncle, of my new assignment. He expressed great concern on my behalf. He said Weerasinghe,[2] the Assistant Superin-tendent I had to work with, was a notorious anti-management trouble maker and union activist. He himself had suffered at the hands of this man who had organized workers to jeer him when he came for work after a dispute with the union and had slogans painted on the warehouse walls insulting him. He advised me to go back to the Captain and decline the offer of the new post.

It was clear to me that I could not lose face by going back to the Captain and declining the new position. I decided that I would work out this situation without guidance from my superiors. As soon as my new position was officially announced in the corporation, I in-vited Weerasinghe to my room. Weerasinghe was a thin man with the stubble of a scruffy beard on his face and a slight scowl when he was in the company of managers. I greeted him by warmly shak-ing his hand and drawing him to a chair and saw a slight hesitant smile illuminate his face. I called the office peon and ordered tea for both of us. I commenced the meeting by leaning forward and saying to him: 'Mr. Weerasinghe, let me say that I am very happy to be able to work with you. I may be an educated man but I know little about port operations and nothing about managing cargo gear. You have done this job for several years and you know everything there is to know on this subject. So I will be guided by you in my work and seek

---

[1] In the 1950s my father had served as the Works Manager of the Governent Factory and it gave me great emotional satisfaction to see his lone, large photo hanging in the main workshop area.

[2] In this instance, I have used the real name of a person.

your advice on all official matters. You will be my teacher about the work in this unit.'

Weerasinghe's face lit up more and he smiled broadly and sincerely while we sipped tea. He responded by saying, 'Sir, you are the first superior I have had in this place who spoke to me sincerely, like a true gentleman. I will do everything I can to help you in this work. I will not fail you.' Thereafter, at several meetings, we worked out our plans. He told me that valuable cargo gear was discarded after any slight damage and new purchases were made because no one was interested in repairing the damage. The men in the unit had experience of repairing gear in the pre-nationalization management era. With some incentive payment, they would carry out repairs and look after the gear stores and prevent theft or wastage. I promised to obtain management approval for extra payments to workers for repairs carried out, which I succeeded in doing without delay. I in turn, worked out a system of documentation and control to ensure that gear was requested in writing by stevedoring units in advance when they made work plans for ships and was returned to the gear stores after work concluded. Wharf Superintendents habitually requested gear just before work started and then failed to return them to gear stores after finishing work on ships, leading to delay in work and loss of gear.

Once these and some other changes were introduced, Weerasinghe took me on tours of the dozen odd gear stores in the port. At each place, he gathered round the workers and eulogized me in a speech, describing me as a very good boss who had the interests of the workers at heart. The men were pleased with their increased remuneration and showed their approval of the new superintendent. I would respond with a short speech, thanking the workers for their cooperation and services and in turn praised my assistant as a very able officer. Within a few months, much to my own astonishment and that of the top management, the unit was functioning more efficiently and at lower costs.

At the end of the year, the Stevedoring Manager was writing his annual assessment of his senior staff. After finishing this work, he gathered them in his room and announced that he would read to them his assessment of my work. He read: 'In my 25 years as an officer in this port, I have not come across a young officer as capable and efficient as Mr. Kenneth....' This elicited mumbled congratulations from the other much older men in the room, though I am certain they resented such heavy praise though they could not express it openly.

The high praise I received publicly from my supervisor had a strong impact on me. It gave me a sense of greater confidence in my own abilities and inspired me to try to innovate in future as well. My loyalty to him was assured. The Stevedoring Manager was a simple man with a good heart, though he was not a particularly able manager. He regarded his boss, the Captain, almost with reverence and followed orders without question. He was a deeply religious Christian Catholic and a very honourable man. Every month, on a Saturday evening, he invited his senior staff to his spacious house in Mutuwal, where his wife laid out an excellent dinner while he plied us with the potent local liquor, arrack. After many drinks, he would become sentimental and call his wife and sons to meet us and describe their virtues, somewhat to their embarrassment.

A few years later, I left the port to advance my career by joining a giant multinational corporation but I never forgot this kind gentleman. Without fail, I sent him a Christmas card and a note every year for two decades till he died, even though in the latter years he had become senile in retirement and never bothered to respond to me. I worked with many able supervisors in later years in the corporate sector but I never met such a fine man who had the capacity to inspire others and win their affection.

Weerasinghe's story also had a happy ending. On my departure, and with my strong recommendation, he was promoted and became superintendent, after which he was a different man without a constant sense of grievance.

4

CLASS AND CASTE SYSTEMS

THE DIVIDE BETWEEN THE MANAGERIAL CLASS AND THE WORKING class that exists in most societies is particularly pronounced in South Asia which has a history of caste based on occupations. In most of South Asia, class and caste are traditional divisions that hinder both social and economic progress. This has created extreme social stratification with the higher castes dominating economic and political life while the lower castes remain under-privileged. It is one of the root causes of the armed rebellions in South Sri Lanka by the Peoples' Liberation Front in 1972 and 1988 and the Liberation Tigers of Tamil Eelam in the North and East from 1975 onwards.

British colonialism further divided the society by adding another layer, whereby every white-skinned European was superior to even the highest coloured native. Fortunately, the nationalist movement that gained ascendancy in Sri Lanka after independence in 1948 began to ridicule some superficial relics of the colonial culture. As the old generation of managers gave way to the new, this mentality underwent a slight change in form but not in substance. The great divide still remains.

This culture of management that prevailed after independence in Sri Lanka needs further explanation. The small number of British expatriates who dominated the enormously large native populations of South Asia succeeded in holding power for so long because they were able to create the illusion that they were the superior race, the governing race. This was a result of carefully developed structures in social, political and economic life. The British held aloof from the native population in a way that earlier Dutch and Portuguese colonisers had not done. By being aloof and by putting on a front before the natives, they were able, to hide their real human weaknesses, like senior army officers in their glorious uniforms parading before their soldiers.

The imperial power controlled the economy and the exchequer, so they lavished much of the wealth on their own people. White British or European expatriates were given the top positions, with salaries and perks far exceeding those of their equivalent native officers, plus luxury bungalows, servants and all-expenses paid 'home leave'. They mixed socially with select native families on formal occasions. Marriage with natives was taboo, unlike the earlier Dutch and Portuguese. They met on evenings in 'Whites Only' social clubs. To be white was to be members of a very superior caste, and the caste system was understood in South Asia. The small minority of wealthy Sri Lankan students who went to Britain for higher studies were in disbelief at their first sight of poor white people begging in the streets of London or living in the slums of large European cities.

New arrivals from Britain were briefed on rules of social conduct before they started work. Mixing freely with the locals would break the illusion of white superiority. It was acceptable to have a native mistress but marrying a native within the country was taboo. We knew of a young British tea plantation manager who fell in love with an attractive local girl of mixed ancestry, the equivalent of the Anglo-Indians, or Burghers as they are called in Sri Lanka. He decided to marry the girl. He was warned by the company. He persisted and lost his job and had to leave the country and reside in England where he married the girl.

The veneration of white people persists in most of South Asia even today. Generations of cultural propaganda have taken a toll on many sections of the population. The impact of this on social and economic development has still to be studied by sociologists.

When the British officers gradually gave way to locals in the public and private sectors after independence, the locals maintained the same colonial traditions and aloofness. Top civil servants were addressed by ordinary people as *hamuduruwo*,[1] an honorific title reserved for the feudal aristocracy in the time of the ancient Sinhala kings of Sri Lanka. They did not socialise with their subordinates and kept the ordinary public at bay. They assumed a pseudo-British accent and drank beer in exclusive social clubs after work and played billiards, tennis or golf while their wives gossiped and arranged bridge or dinner parties. Their children went to exclusive schools and treated students from other schools, particularly Buddhist schools, with condescension. The top sports tournaments were played only among the elite secondary schools. All this had a corrupting influence on the minds of the managerial class in post-colonial society.

A brilliant civil servant and scholar of this era, now deceased, related to me a story of his entry to the civil service in the 1940s. Having achieved a First Class Honours degree from the University of Ceylon, he secured a place in the Civil Service after succeeding in the competitive Civil Service examinations and was posted to a city in the South named Galle as a cadet. The Office Assistant of the *kachcheri*,[2] who is the non-executive head of the clerical and other subordinate staff, was aghast that the new cadet had studied in a Buddhist secondary school and was not from an elite Colombo school and treated him with disdain.

Another incident worth relating occurred in 1958 and involved my supervisor in the big subsidiary of the foreign multinational corporation that I worked with. After 1956, the government began to restrict the number of expatriate managers a foreign-owned company could bring. So he was recruited by the company as its first local manager. He had worked previously in the public service as a senior manager. When he went for his first lunch at the Senior Managers'

---

[1] The English equivalent would be Your Lordship.
[2] *Kachcheri* is the appellation for the provincial government headquarters in Sri Lanka.

canteen the rest of the managers, all expatriate British and white-skinned, walked away and complained to the Chairman that they could not be expected to sit for lunch with a coloured native. The chairman reminded them that the political climate in the country had changed and that if they did not like the new situation it would be their turn to leave the country.

These social pressures weighed on the native Sri Lankan managers of the early post-independence era, both in the public and private sectors. There was the need to gain acceptance in a hierarchy that was tainted with snobbery. Some were able to maintain their personality and self respect, but others were constantly trying to gain acceptance through servility to their white superiors, while being harsh and overbearing in their relations with subordinates. Naturally, this made some of them weak managers and also contributed to the high level of labour unrest that prevailed in the two decades after independence.

Two laudable features of the local senior public service managers in this early post-independence period must be noted. They were invariably scrupulously honest in financial matters. They considered themselves part of the old British tradition and were proud of this special status. If public service salaries were not sufficient to maintain their superior social status, they could marry the daughters of rich business people and thus gain sizeable dowries. High government officials and, to a lesser degree, top corporate managers of foreign companies, were always in demand in the marriage market because of their social status and authority.

Another admirable feature of senior civil servants of this era was their unwillingness to accommodate corrupt local politicians. The prestige of the service, derived from the British colonial era, was strong enough to intimidate their political bosses. Alas, that prestige eroded within a decade of independence, with elected politicians assuming the privileges of pre-colonial feudal chiefs, and the consequences were again unfortunate for the country.

Working in the port as a stevedoring superintendent, with about 1,400 workers in the unit (which, by the way, was the smallest stevedoring unit in the port), I began to recognize the innate decency and humanity of the rough port worker. With this growing maturity, perhaps, I was able to mingle with them at work and feel comfortable in their company, which in turn made them open and friendly towards me. I began to recognize their desire to survive as human beings in their difficult circumstances and they recognized the limits of my authority as a supervisor.

A few incidents will illustrate how they tried to show their approval. One morning, as I was seated in my stevedoring unit office, Labour Supervisor Pius arrived for work with a distraught look and told me as he signed the attendance register, 'Sir, someone picked my pocket while I was walking through Pettah on my way to work. I have lost my money'. Now, the Baghdad Stevedoring Unit office was not a fancy place. It was an old wooden structure with faded light blue paint and the superintendent's desk was near an open window that looked out into the waterfront. From my seat, I could hear the conversations of the workers who milled around the open area before and after work. This enabled me to be familiar with some of their names and faces. On hearing the news, Mr K, an Assistant Superintendent who often tried to ingratiate himself to me by being at my side, came up and said, 'Sir, you know Sumathipala who hangs around near the office and talks to you at times. He is the leader of the Pettah pickpockets. Why not ask him?'

I sent a message to the ship where Sumathipala was working, asking him to meet me after work. When he came to see me in the evening, I told him casually, 'Sumathipala, Pius Mahaththaya[3] has lost his purse today in the Pettah. Can you help him?' The next morning, Sumathipala handed the purse to me, contents intact. The subject was closed.

There was another notorious character who worked in the unit as a stevedore. He was nicknamed Bomba Piyadasa because his second job was making hand bombs that were sold or used on contract jobs when he was hired by people in his neighbourhood to

[3] Mahattaya is a Sinhala equivalent of Mister.

kill or maim people. One day, to show his appreciation, he told me that if any of my enemies were bothering me, he would be happy to 'give them the works'. I told him kindly, 'Piyadasa, I have no enemies'. 'That is wonderful. It is because you are a good gentleman'.

Finally, when I left the port to join a multinational corporation and advance my career, the labour union officials organized a farewell dinner at Pillau's Restaurant in the Pettah, famed for its biriyani rice and chicken curry, with dozens of cases of fiery arrack that loosened tongues and a torrent of laudatory speeches. I value the photos of the farewell given to me after this event as a sign of the decency of the often maligned port worker.

Conventional management training does not teach managers how to interact on a human level with labour. The dry theories on how to motivate workers are fundamentally flawed as these have a narrow focus: they assume that the workers are either concerned with more money or are striving for more recognition from their bosses for good work. In this management thinking, workers are another input for production, purchased at the best price and discarded whenever the management deems they are a superfluous cost. It does not recognize that workers are human beings who would want to have a human interaction with the management or owners who hire them for their work. This divide, which is fostered by management as it creates its own elite society removed from the ordinary world of the 'common man', is often an underlying cause of industrial unrest and lost productivity.

GOOD GOVERNANCE
and WEAK MANAGERS

Guard against arrogance. For anyone in a leading position, this is a matter of principle and an important condition for maintaining unity. Even those who have made no serious mistakes and have achieved very great success in their work should not be arrogant. Celebration of the birthdays of Party leaders is forbidden. Naming places, streets and enterprises after Party leaders is likewise forbidden. We must keep to our style of plain living and hard work and put a stop to flattery and exaggerated praise.

—Chairman Mao Zedong

From Chairman Mao Zedong's concluding speech at the Second Plenary Session of the 7th Central Committee Meeting of the Communist Party of China on 13 March 1949. The communists under Mao had recently defeated the Kuomintang and taken over China, with the active support of Chinese workers and peasants. This is from the 11th of 12 guidelines he laid out for party leaders in governing the New China. From the chapter on 'Methods of Work of Party Committees', in *Selected Readings from the Works of Mao Tse-Tung*, Foreign Language Press, Peking, China, 1971.

5

THE GREAT DIVIDE IN A BUSINESS

THE LARGE ANGLO-AMERICAN MULTINATIONAL CORPORATION THAT totally dominates the lucrative tobacco market in Sri Lanka advertised for management trainees in 1963. The excise duty revenue from the corporation is a sizeable part of government revenue and hence restrictions on tobacco have never been seriously implemented in the country. To be hired by such a company as a manager was the ambition of most aspiring young middle-class youth at the time. Around 450 young men (no women, please, that was the fashion at the time) who were in the University of Ceylon in my time had applied for the three positions advertised. After sifting through these applications, the company called about 60 of us for the first interview. At the end of six interviews, conducted mainly by comparatively young British managers assisted by the Sri Lankan Personnel Manager, there were nine of us left. The interviews were in the posh offices of the company in Colombo and focused on the usual educational and work achievements plus an assessment of the poise, personality, dress and English language accents of the candidates.

The final interview was a lunch at the Jubilee Room of the Galle Face Hotel, then the best luncheon address in town. Here, the candidates dressed in lounge suits made small talk with the white British directors and senior managers over beer or dry sherry to prove their upper class social skills and display their best table manners. At the end of all this, three of us were chosen: apart from me, there was an executive in the Central Bank (a good choice) and the other was a person who had, in my time, been dismissed from our university hall of residence and de-barred from lectures for irrational violence towards fellow students. His final act was when he raided the locked room of a respected senior student, who had done him no harm, and deliberately cut up his clothes with sharp scissors. The only possible reason for his selection was that he was a good rugby football player for a club where most of the members were expatriate British managers.

Disillusioned by this experience, I shared my thoughts with the other successful candidate from the Central Bank. He expressed his reservations about the all-white British composition of the existing management and their social attitudes. We both declined the job offer, much to the consternation of the Personnel Manager who wondered whether we were in our right minds.

Two years later I was interviewed for the position of a Senior Manager in marketing by the local subsidiary of another giant multinational corporation that dominated consumer products manufacturing and marketing in the country. Let's call this multinational XYZ International Limited and call the local subsidiary XYZ Ceylon Limited. Here, a shift in culture was already visible, as the government had by then restricted the number of expatriate managers that a business could bring in. Instead of young men training for higher jobs in Britain by working in the ex-colonies, the newly recruited local top management people were mature middle-aged men drawn from senior public service positions. These six interviews were not concluded with formal lunches or dinners. Instead, after a process of interviews, I emerged out of the 400 odd applicants for the position.

One of the points in my favour was that I had managed a stevedoring unit with 1,400 workers, which was a number slightly in excess of the work force in this company at the time. But, the interview panels were also able to extract information in a subtle manner regarding the candidates' families (are they socially acceptable?) and their high school background (are they from the elite schools we send our children to?). The university was not an issue, as there was only one university in the country at the time but being an actor in the University English Dramatic Club was possibly a point in my favour (was that better than being an actor in the Sinhala or Tamil Drama societies?). Holding elected office in university student unions (I had been President of the University Students' Council, my hall of residence and the Socialist Society) could have been a definite disadvantage a few years earlier but, in the current political climate, it was regarded as evidence of mere youthful folly. University student unions in the fifties and sixties were sometimes centres of non-violent student agitation, unlike the violent agitations of later decades.

Companies in Sri Lanka still go to great lengths to establish the exclusiveness of the managerial class that was created in colonial times. This is evident in the culture of the multinational corporations in Sri Lanka. Managers wear neckties and are chauffeur driven to office in company cars. Non-management staff and workers are less formally attired and come to work by public transport. Workers may even be required to wear garish uniforms supplied by the company to accentuate their humble status. Even factory managers mostly direct work from air-conditioned offices and send down orders to the factory floor through supervisors, like the British Army officers who sent orders to the rank and file through junior officers and platoon sergeants. Managers ate four course meals in a separate dining area with liveried waiters for service while supervisors, salesmen and workers ate humbler meals in separate canteens served buffet style. Managers are paid club-membership fees to encourage them to patronize the posh Golf Club or other expensive social clubs which are beyond the means of the ordinary person.

Parading these class symbols and the divide it created perhaps accounted for the fact that multinational corporations, even while paying much higher salaries to employees and providing better working conditions than ordinary national firms, had more labour unrest than the national norm. During my 14 years in XYZ Ceylon Ltd., there were numerous strikes, some lasting as long as three months, during the course of which managers were jeered and sometimes even assaulted by angry workers.

Long after I left the Port Cargo Corporation, I began to consider how port workers and other employees in large workplaces could be organised for better productivity, given that trade unions would continue to be militant because of the political framework within which they operated in Sri Lanka. I only had vague ideas on this subject while I was working in the port: my knowledge of management was too limited at the time. Small firms do not face much difficulty in managing its few employees: the boss is always a presence and every employee is under close surveillance. Any employee stepping out of line could be rewarded, punished or dismissed. A small workforce has little ability to make a united protest. New recruits could be easily found to replace them. But a militant workforce of about 40,000 is another matter. And the issue remains to be understood as this is not a problem peculiar to the port authorities in Sri Lanka of a past era: it is an ever present issue in Sri Lanka and many developing countries.

The military was the first institution in the world which developed systems that enabled it to recruit large numbers of normal people to willingly perform the most unpleasant tasks for a comparatively low level of remuneration. Through uniforms, badges of rank, daily parades, bugles, trumpets, flags, regimental insignia and other ritualised ceremonial activities, plus regular and intensive training, rigid codes of conduct and, above all, by creating a pride in the job by sentimental appeals to glory and patriotism, militaries succeed in sending intelligent men to happily kill total strangers or get killed in the process without much thought of the consequences. Human beings, to some extent like honey bees or ants, can be regimented to the extent that they cease to think like human beings and act almost like automatons. Perhaps North Korean society provided such an example. But that should not be a model for humanity in normal social relations.

Military practices cannot be fully introduced into workplaces and God forbid that it should be. But there are surely better ways of getting people to work with a will without excessive dependence on rule books and disciplinary codes which dictate punishments for infringement of orders, and praise and minor rewards for exceptionally good performance. In short, it is the carrot and stick method used by people who train animals to perform in a circus. The modern Japanese automobile corporations were pioneers in developing systems where large numbers of workers performed at exceptionally high levels of productivity and quality control by recognising the workers' human dignity and innate abilities and innovative skills. People sometimes tend to think that these cannot be replicated because, they say, and this is not said as a compliment, the Japanese are an extraordinary people. But this has been done by Japanese auto companies with the same level of success in South Asia as in the USA. However few other organizations are willing to learn from these successes and change their ways.

In 1988 I participated as a resource person in a training programme for public enterprise managers in Kuala Lumpur, Malaysia, organised by the UK Commonwealth Secretariat for Commonwealth countries. Another resource person at these training workshops was a Mr Baghwan, Managing Director of Maruti, an Indian automobile company jointly owned by the Indian government and Suzuki Motors of Japan. He described how Japanese management systems had helped his company in India to achieve high levels of productivity and quality control, making Maruti the leader of this sector in India. It intrigued me because labour management relations throughout South Asia are, essentially, no different from the situation in Sri Lanka. When I expressed my astonishment, he invited me to visit his factory which was situated close to Delhi.

The next year, I was at the Indian Institute of Management in Ahmedabad in Gujarat as a resource person on the same Commonwealth program for public sector top managers from Commonwealth countries. After my work there, I went to Delhi and phoned Mr Baghwan who invited me to come for a tour of the factory. What I saw there was an eye opener. To begin with, Mr Baghwan wore the same uniform, a light blue shirt with the company logo on the shirt pocket and blue trousers, as all the other employees. He said that he even attended government meetings in this uniform, while others wore business suits, as it was a symbol of company pride. In the factory, there were no separate rooms or cubicles for managers and other senior staff. Each department sat in a large open hall and the director of the department sat at a table at one end of the open hall. People interacted freely in this communal space. There were separate conference rooms adjoining the hall to be used by groups for meetings.

I went with one of the directors for lunch in the common canteen. Employees, irrespective of rank, were provided with meals during work shifts by the company in a large hall that catered to over a thousand employees. There were three types of standard meals: North Indian, South Indian and Chinese. I opted to sit with a small group of line workers and learnt how proud they were to work in the company. Employees were recruited from all parts of India through competitive selection procedures. Since the remuneration was much higher than the industry standard and the work-place was congenial, the workers faces represented the diversity of the people of India.

In the factory, work was organised as in Japan. Workers came in company buses to the work area half an hour before the start of a shift. They then performed callisthenics to music and had a quick meeting with their team leader on the previous day's performance and the performance target for the day. All work was done by fixed teams, each responsible for one section of the moving production line. If there were absentees, the rest of the team covered up for the deficiency and even the foreman joined the work team when a member had to take a short break to visit the lavatory or have a drink of water from the nearby water filter. At the end of the large assembly area were huge boards on the wall that registered the daily work performances of the workshop in bold figures for all to see. Workers in India evidently had the same human qualities as Japanese workers and invidious distinctions based on nationality were apparently untrue.

It occurred to me that I had striven to achieve some similar results with a few of these methods in my earlier work as Chairman of
the State Timber Corporation of Sri Lanka in the period 1979–81.
But I must confess that I had not developed my management insights to the same degree as I witnessed at the Maruti plant at that
later date. But that is another story which will come in later chapters.

6

SOMETIMES, MANAGERS
ARE TOO HUMAN

As BEFITS A PRESTIGIOUS MULTINATIONAL CORPORATION, XYZ
Ceylon Limited was different from the Port of Colombo in every
visible aspect. The elegant modern buildings were air-conditioned,
well lighted and tastefully furnished. Smartly dressed and attractive
young women paraded around, as secretaries and receptionists, waft-
ing perfumes into the air around. Men in the management offices wore
neckties and spoke in low voices: quite unlike the noisy port where
everyone seemed to be shouting to each other. There was a seeming
order and method in management. Corporate plans, production
plans, sales plans, purchasing plans, financial plans, personnel plans,
product development plans and review meetings for each of these
abounded. No wonder the local competition was disappearing and
the company had gained a monopoly in the markets it worked in.

The genteel atmosphere required that I forget some of the
habits from my port days. When an assistant manager working for
me showed some impertinence, perhaps to test my mettle as a newcomer, I told him off in a manner he would not forget. Later, I was
cautioned by my supervisor, the Director[1], who was also his kinsman,

---

[1] Directors of foreign multinationals are not Directors in the real sense. They
are senior managers who are allocated one share in the company for the period
of their office to support this title. XYZ Ceylon Limited was typically a 100 per
cent foreign-owned subsidiary of XYZ International Limited.

that managers in the company did not use strong language of that kind.

But politics is an essential feature of life in every large corporation. This is not limited to the competition for career advancement or salaries. Human greed and vanity, which all great religious leaders of the past have decried, are still potent human failings. Managers compete for larger rooms, better office furniture, larger carpets, wall hangings, more secretaries, bigger automobiles and every other symbol of managerial snobbery, including closer social contact with higher management. A fast route to promotion is often obsequious behaviour in relations with higher managers. Dare to think independently and tell the superior that he or she could be wrong and you may risk subtle forms of punishment, for a start.

While out of favour with my supervisor in my later years, even as the head of a key department, I was banished from my larger office to a small room in a corner of the office building, next to the tea room, and my full time secretary was withdrawn in favour of a pool secretary that I had to request for daily. Being cynical of office politics by then, I raised no protests but expressed satisfaction (to give no satisfaction to the superior) and even greatly enjoyed the privacy provided in this obscure corner of the building which allowed me to work independently according to my own rules.

Two, true life examples will illustrate the mentality of the aspiring manager. Expatriate company chairmen of XYZ Ceylon Ltd. came from UK and went away every four years. These men (always men, again, no ladies please) were generally of two kinds. Some were middle-level managers in the great hierarchy of the international corporation that had its subsidiaries in about 85 countries, who were destined for promotion and needed to gain some experience of running a company by cutting their teeth in the less important markets in Asia or Africa. Others were middling managers of middling competence who were reaching the age of retirement and needed a more glorified position in a less important market as a retirement gift for long and loyal service.

Every Sri Lankan expatriate Chairman of XYZ Ceylon Ltd. had a different personality and it was truly wonderful to see so many senior managers trying to change their personalities to suit the style of a new boss and gain his attention. For example, if the Chairman was a keen golfer, more managers would be seen in the Royal Colombo Golf Club links around the time favoured by the boss. When one Chairman only indulged in sailing, some managers went to the enormous expense of investing in sailing boats and joined the sailing club. Others, of the less sporty variety, sought identification through similar club neckties or reading material. However, unlike in the case of many local bosses, there is little evidence that these expatriates, from a different cultural milieu, were taken in by these Oriental forms of adoration. On the whole, they were fair minded and ignored the class, caste, family and other ties that were so beloved of the natives.

Flattery is an art form in most of South Asia, sought after and often readily given, embedded in the past traditions of that society. Superiors expect their subordinates in the workplaces to humble themselves in their presence, flatter them and even perform menial services like shopping for their wives and doing other household chores. Philip Baldeus, the perceptive Dutch writer who lived in India and Ceylon in Dutch times wrote a detailed account of Dutch relations with the Sinhalese kings in 1672.[2] He described how the Dutch were able occupy the ports and coastal belts of the country and extract their wealth, in defiance of all treaty agreements, simply by humbling themselves and crawling on the floor in the royal presence, indulging in extravagant flattery and giving them exotic gifts. The Dutch avoided open conflict and expensive wars but gained what they wanted by describing themselves as obedient servants of the Sinhalese king who were protecting his interests, while illegally occupying the rich coastal lands and denying the king access to his own ports and to foreign commerce.

A Sales Manager working in my department was an old friend from my student days. Ameen had been an excellent high school

---

[2] 'A True and Exact Description of the Most Celebrated East India Coasts of Malabar and Coromandel as also of the Isle of Ceylon', Philip Baldeus, Amsterdam, 1671, re-printed by Asian Educational Services, New Delhi, Madras, 1998.

cadet[3] sergeant and had won the Queen's Cup for the best rifle shot in the army junior rifle shooting championships. He had joined the company as a salesman, was good at his job and after two decades of good work, was promoted to Area Sales Manager. During his first briefing by the General Sales Manager, he was told that one of his tasks, on returning to Colombo from the weekly tour of his sales area, was to stop at a hill-country meat market and collect the 20 pounds of special beef that a butcher prepared for the chairman of the company and to deliver it personally to the Chairman's bungalow. Ameen, being an independent and self-respecting man, protested that this was not part of his job. His supervisor countered that it was an order from the Director that was beyond questioning.

Ameen, obstinate fellow that he was, went to the butcher's shop on his way back from the sales tour and told the butcher to pack the meat in a box and send it by railway, addressed to the Chairman's residence. Three days later, the Chairman's household received a note from the Station Master of the Colombo Fort Railway Station that there was a putrid smelling parcel addressed to the Chairman at the station and that the health authorities had ordered it to be destroyed and that the costs were being charged to him.

There was consternation in the office of the Director. Few knew of this extraordinary form of personal service to the expatriate Chairman's wife by the Director but now the cat was out of the bag of tricks. Subordinate staff had difficulty reaching the boss the next day as the Director was busy apologizing to the Chairman's wife on the phone and promising to make amends. Ameen's career was finished. Shortly after, he left the company and joined another company as a Sales Manager.

There are penalties for failure to pay obeisance to those fickle gods and seek their guidance. At the end of a year, I had prepared the evaluation of my immediate subordinate staff and sent it to the

[3] High school cadets are students who do some elementary military training during a week-end each month and receive two weeks annual training by the Sri Lanka Army. It is aimed at interesting young men to join the military services on leaving school. In reality, very few took this next step.

Director. While reviewing my assessments, he disagreed with my glowing tributes to the highest performing Product Manager in my division. A dedicated manager who was a top achiever, Nihal was an independent personality who could be argumentative in his dealings with superiors. I had no problem with that. But the Director obviously had a problem and he called him to the meeting in my presence and told him that he disagreed with my assessment and that he was unfit for higher office as his educational qualifications did not include a university degree. The man left the company later and set up a small business which was very successful.

On the other hand, never forget that promotions may come easily if you are a blood relative of the boss. On another occasion, I had praised the work of a junior manager who was performing a limited role in a niche function. I was summoned by the Director who demanded to know why I had not recommended him for promotion to senior management. I responded that the man had not even obtained the ordinary school certificate (Ordinary Levels), had no writing skills, and was incapable of analyzing and conceptualizing business situations. He responded with 'I will not hear the end of it from my family if I don't promote him.' The junior manager was his first cousin. He was promoted. After a while the man left the company, weary of the criticisms of his performance by his superiors.

Office politics works in mysterious ways and those outside the charmed circles are often caught unawares in traps. One of my early positions was that of Product Manager/Toilet Preparations. This meant that I monitored and supervised the market performance of various brands of toilet preparations manufactured and marketed by the company and proposed schemes to higher management for improving sales and profits through appropriate marketing strategies. The major product group in my section was toothpaste, where the company had three international brands. Over the last five years, the company sales of this product had slowly eroded. Reading the company product assessments prepared for the head office in London, I learnt that the total market was declining due to weakening economic conditions in the country. This position was backed by the market research prepared bi-annually by the company's market research unit.

I took over the raw market research data from the Market Research Manager and after a week of number crunching, mostly at home, concluded that the market research findings were at variance with the data collected. The market was growing and this was coming from the main competitor who was growing at the expense of the company's main brand and also expanding the market.

Based on these findings, I re-wrote the analysis and the strategy and gave this to my then immediate superior, the Company Marketing Manager. The innocent man was also new at this job and was very impressed. He wrote 'Excellent Analysis' on the report and took it to the Director and was shocked when he was reproached for being disloyal and ordered to stop such unsolicited analyses in future. (Market research is sometimes designed to prove, I learnt, what the genius in the boss had already discovered.) Toothpastes, thereafter, continued to decline till the company was compelled to re-launch the existing brands with new formulations, packaging and a new strategy, recommended by the visiting regional director from the London office. After that the company's market shares soared and the market itself took off dramatically.

Another brand had a less happy ending. Hair cream was also declining in sales and I felt that the brand needed a more modern image. The advertising agency worked on a new advertising campaign based on visuals that I obtained from the London office for the brand. These were shown to the director for final approval. He had a better idea. He pulled out a set of old visuals that featured him as the male model, in his younger days as a manager when he had a full head of hair. The brand declined further and was withdrawn from the market on the instructions of a new results-conscious expatriate chairman.

These misadventures were dwarfed by the magnificent disaster that XYZ Ceylon Ltd. went through a few years later. It was, as the company later assessed in its evaluation and explanation to the head office in London, a valuable learning experience, a contention that I was willing to endorse for different reasons. Sri Lanka is a poor country and, at that time, in the nineteen sixties, was even poorer. Expatriate British managers, working in their cocoons in air-conditioned offices, spending pleasant evenings in posh clubs with their families and living in large bungalows maintained by a dozen servants who pampered them from the wake-up bed tea to the late night nightcap, could hardly imagine the life of the ordinary citizen in a Third World country.

There were numerous suggestions made about the need for sophisticated perfumes, after-shave lotions and other expensive luxury items that the corporate group's European companies made for their sophisticated markets. But barely 1 per cent of the households in the country had an income level comparable to that of the average middle class family in Europe and that number amounted to about 32,000 households. As a Product Manager who should have initiated projects based on these bold suggestions, I was a failure. All these suggestions were ignored and I did not care to repeatedly explain the marketing rationale for my attitude after a while.

But others in my position saw great opportunities. An expatriate British chairman was astonished by the number of coconuts consumed daily in the average Sri Lankan household. All Sri Lankan curries and most cooked foods have coconut milk. Early morning, people wake up to the ritual sound of coconuts being cracked in the neighbouring households as breakfast is prepared. What a drudgery this labour was, he contended. So much labour, to crack the coconuts, shred the kernel with a hand-held scraper and then to extract the milk by squeezing the scrapings by hand with a little water. All this done manually! Instant coconut milk was the answer.

His subordinates, from the directors down, rallied to the cause to save the Sri Lankan housewife all this misery. There was no need for feasibility studies. The market was waiting and project proposals were rushed through. From Directors to Marketing Manager to the Product Manager/Foods, the sales estimates and profit figures were moved up and down and with each passing the numbers grew. It was announced that the market covered the entire 3.3 million house-holds in the country. The Chairman summoned meetings to inform the management of the new project that would transform the company and the food market in the country. The directors weighed in by asserting that the product would lead to the creation of a separate company to deal exclusively with the product which could over-shadow the present company in size and profitability. They promised that this would open up a number of promotional prospects for the existing middle management.

There was now no time to expend on massive product develop-ment research, as was the company procedure. The Technical Director's staff that supervised the Development Section produced samples of the product. It was an oily cream packed in a carton. The cream had to be dissolved in water to produce the coconut milk. Pre launch advertising was already prepared to alert the public to the new pro-duct that was soon sampled to housewives by sampling teams in several key towns. Full-page newspaper advertisements showed huge bunches of coconuts being transformed into ready-made coconut milk that was so convenient to use.

Dealers and brokers in coconut wholesaling arrived in the com-pany offices with offers of sustainable supplies of fresh coconuts at competitive prices. But the company was not entertaining such offers. Instead, trucks from the port were bringing in dairy milk powder in bulk packages. These were made into a paste with water and a little coconut oil and coconut flavour and this was stabilized by chemicals and packed to make this new wonder 'coconut' product in strict secrecy.

I was not involved in this operation except as an observer. The company had an Outdoor Promotions unit that I had once headed. One of its tasks was the product sampling operation. About 220 trained young women, divided into work teams under a supervisor, visited households in selected sample market areas to demonstrate a product to the housewives and sell it at a discounted price to en-courage purchase. This was particularly useful before test marketing as it provided a feedback on the acceptance of a product by house-wives after repeated use over a period of time.

I happened to talk to some of these supervisors during a casual social encounter and asked them about the revolutionary new product. They were unanimous that the product was unacceptable. During the first sampling round, several middle class housewives in urban areas who had seen so many publicity advertisements had bought the product. During the second round they had complained that it was too expensive because it did not provide the claimed equivalent of six coconuts. More disturbing, the product broke down in texture and tasted different from the real thing. During the third round of sampling, many of the sampling girls were abused and shown the door for distributing a bad product with false claims. Had the supervisors brought these problems to the attention of their manager? The answer was yes.

Concerned about the effect of all this on the huge investments being made in the product, I met my director and expressed my worries, assuming he was misinformed by his subordinates. The answer was a shocker: 'This is the Chairman's pet project. I am not going to bell the cat. You do it, if you feel up to it.' I was not up to it. It was not my business.

The product was launched nationally with much fanfare, backed by the most extravagant advertising for a company product to that date. The product was a complete flop. It was withdrawn a few months later with heavy costs. Then cheerful assessments of how much the company had gained through this valuable learning experience were being circulated to the head offices in UK. The subordinate management was told at meetings that the product was ahead of its time and would have a great place in the future years.

But a fundamental flaw at the core of the product concept, quite apart from the badly performing product itself, was never discussed. A unit of the product was three times the price of the equivalent number of fresh coconuts it sought to replace. So it would only appeal to the wealthier upper middle class, if at all. But all upper middle class houses in Sri Lanka have several servants to do domestic work because rural poverty provides an endless source of very cheap household help. The upper middle class housewife does not cook. She has a 'cook woman', familiarly called *kussi amma*, literally meaning 'kitchen mother', to do that menial task. She sees no reason to provide convenience products at a higher cost 'to encourage idleness among the servants'.

Now, do you believe that the authors and participants in this fiasco suffered in their career prospects because of the enormous loss to the company? Think again. The Product Manager who worked on the new product was promoted to Marketing Manager/Foods, a new post specially created by splitting the job of his existing supervisor, the Company Marketing Manager, for the advancement of a loyal man. The Factory Manager who developed the failed product became General Production Manager, still later the Technical Director and finally the Vice-Chairman of the company. This provides a valuable lesson for the aspiring manager. The shortest path to career advancement is usually reserved for the unrepentant cheerleader for the boss.

7

SEARCHING FOR TRANSPARENCY

LACK OF TRANSPARENCY, A EUPHEMISM USED IN MANAGEMENT AND economic writings for corruption in business, politics or government, is today a major issue. International aid agencies proclaim that aid will be withheld or minimized unless governments in developing countries tackle corruption. One of the arguments for the privatization of state assets, apart from the widely acknowledged view that governments are poor business managers, is that the private sector tends to be more transparent in comparison to the public sector. This division of people into two different species, public sector animals and private sector animals, has gained so much credence that I often unconsciously tend to this orthodox view.

Low-level bribery is visible in the public sector in Sri Lanka, as in many developing countries. Poorly paid peons or clerks in government offices may want a '*santhosam*'[1] of a few rupees to pass on applications for government documents for processing or to retrieve them when a person goes for collection of these. In the Port of Colombo, at the time I worked there, it was customary for customers to place 25 cents on the table of a warehouse clerk when collecting documents to clear the goods (the rupee was worth much more at the time and 25 cents was not to be laughed at and would be about

[1]Literally, an expression of satisfaction by the recipient in the form of a reward.

US$1.0 in current money). No words on the subject were exchanged as all parties knew the correct form. Shippers and shipping agents sent cases of whisky to senior port officials at Christmas and were very upset if these were refused as this was taken as a sign of a loss of favour with the official. But such practices were not supposed to take place in large private sector companies, least of all in prestigious multinational corporations.

The energetic do-gooder in middle management, I discovered, is often a fool. It pays to humbly seek the guidance of the supervisor in most office matters. It does not pay to take initiatives with the idea of improving business profitability on your own. While working as the Product Manager/Toilet Preparations in the multinational corporation, I was tasked with a major product development effort to upgrade baby products: improving the product and its packaging, new advertising, etc, based on successfully tested models from another market region of the international corporate group. Samples of packaging and product arrived from the UK offices. While the Product Development personnel (some of them were exceptionally dedicated and competent people) worked on product improvement, the Buying Department worked on obtaining suppliers to make the new packaging.

The baby talcum powder package proved to be a difficult task. It was made of moulded plastic that was made in the country by a few firms at the time. At the monthly product development review meeting, the Buying Manager handling packaging tabled a sample of the new pack and said it would cost Rs 1.06. I was aghast. A quick calculation showed me that this would bring the retail price of the product to Rs 3.75, whereas the market leader, a competitive international brand also in a moulded plastic pack, was retailed at Rs 1.75. I said that this price was unacceptable. The Buying Manager said this was the best price obtainable and he knew the packaging market. Everyone around the table felt there was no choice: the price of the product would have to go up sharply to accommodate the cost.

I came back to my desk and thought of the consequences. If the price was beyond twice that of the market leader, the brand would become history, and the product manager would be a convenient scapegoat. I took the Yellow Pages and ran through the list of potential suppliers. I rang up the biggest manufacturer of moulded plastics, a company owned by a well known Parsi[2] businessman. I drove to his office, put the sample from UK on his table and asked him for a quote. He asked me what my company was. When I told him, he said he would not talk to buyers from the company as they always demanded substantial kickbacks. He didn't want their business. I told him I was not a buyer but the marketing person developing the brand and that I did not want any commissions. He then phoned the company to verify my credentials and said he would contact me later and kept the control sample.

Three weeks later, just prior to the next monthly product development meeting, I got the control sample and his excellent manufactured sample and a quote of Rs 0.46 for a pack for the quantity we required. I went to the development meeting elated and, when the turn came, laid out my sample and quotation. There was consternation all around. The Director/Buying started by saying that marketing personnel had no authority to visit buyers and the Buying Manager protested at this interference with his work. I was isolated, looking like a thief who has been caught red-handed. The expatriate Chairman spoke in measured words and said he would deal with this issue later. The meeting moved on to the next subject. A few days later, all marketing managers received a brief note from the Chairman saying they were not permitted to contact suppliers on their own initiative: that was the job of the Buyers.

But the story did not end there. At the next development meeting, that particular Buying Manager proudly announced that his own supplier had also agreed to bring the price of the pack down to Rs 0.46. Congratulations were in order for his good work.

Do-gooders are in many respects incurable fools. Shortly after, I was at a dinner party where I met a manager working in the printing

---

[2] The Parsis are a distinct group in India and Sri Lanka. They were originally refugees from Persia fleeing the persecution of Zoroastrians by the Muslims many centuries ago.

business in the country. This company was part of one of the largest
public quoted companies in the country. I innocently asked him
why he did not supply our company that was, after all, the biggest
consumer products company in the country. He answered that our
company buyers were crooks who wanted high commissions of the
sort he was not authorized to offer. I was offended and told him
that his company would get the business if their prices were right.
I later sent him samples of the toothpaste cartons we marketed as
toothpaste was a leading product line. Shortly after, the quotations
for these arrived and these were found to be lower than the existing
buying prices of the company. I had now learnt that buyers were
far more powerful than marketing managers in the company, for
reasons that were not very clear. So I went to the concerned Buying
Manager for print material. He was a shrewd elderly man who used
his charm to work out of difficulties, unlike his colleague who used
hostility to fight his way out of problems. He told me he was very
happy that the biggest printing company in the business, for once,
was willing to offer good prices. Perhaps they wanted to please me
as a new marketing man. He said he would transfer a part of the
toothpaste carton business to this company to see how things worked
out. So there the issue rested. I did not want to push my luck further
on this issue.

But, as I have said, do-gooders have a mental kink that does not
allow them to rest. I knew, most of the company knew, and suppliers
knew that being in the Buying Department of the company was a
lucrative business. Salesmen in my department, when I became a
head of department, would tell me in jest that they did not want
promotion to management but a transfer to the Buying Department
as clerks. I knew that a lot of our print material was bought at ex-
orbitant costs. So I contacted the chairman of the large corporation
that owned the printing company and he, in turn, sent a letter to the
chairman of our company to note that his printing people offered
the best quality and competitive prices and he would like to see some
business between the two companies for their mutual benefit. This
put our chairman in a spot and he then sent a note to the buyers that

quotations should also be obtained from this printer when printing jobs were sought. Thereafter, some printing jobs were allocated to this company on the basis of their competitive prices.

Transparency, or the lack of it, in the public sector, is far more visible and will be taken up in a later chapter. But corruption and thieving I found are as common to private and public sectors, as it is to less developed as well as highly developed rich nations. What is lacking in a developing country is the mechanism for highlighting such abuses: there is an absence of investigative media reporting and conscientious local shareholders who could act as useful corporate watchdogs.

8

CROSSING THE CLASS BARRIER

MOST SUCCESSFUL CORPORATIONS ARE NOT NECESSARILY BRILLIANT in all areas. There are usually one or two departments that excel and carry the business through; the success of these is the result of the leadership of an excellent manager who is in charge. In XYZ Ceylon Ltd, it was the outstanding excellence of the sales department that gave the company much of its market leadership and this was largely the work of its Sales Director. This man was one of the most dynamic managers I have encountered in this business.

A burly man, who was always in physical movement as befitted his temperament, he set his goals and sales targets very high and demanded the utmost from his subordinates. At the same time, he was generous with his remuneration and conditions of service, lavish in his praise when it was due and constantly in contact with his men in the field to check on their results and difficulties. He talked fast and moved fast. His sales managers and salesmen were driven to work harder and harder. He would have been seen as a bully if he was another man but his managers and sales people loved him and considered him their hero.

He was kind and generous when the occasion demanded it. His managers wanted desks at their homes to write their weekly reports. He told them they could order them from the best furniture dealer in the country at company expense. They wanted typewriters for their use at home. These were given, as well as Thermos flasks to carry hot tea while travelling. They were encouraged to use the company expense account every week to entertain their salesmen and their families for a dinner to bind them into a happy team.

He regularly entertained his managers for an evening beer but this was sometimes a mixed blessing. On Saturday mornings, after returning from an exhausting weeklong sales tour, the sales managers would find the director's car at their doorstep with an invitation from him for beer at his house. This was not good news. Those who were gathered for drinks were then told, after one or two glasses, that sales performances were mediocre during the last week and the managers needed to travel the same day to specified areas to ensure a few big wholesale orders from business houses he had identified in advance to meet the weekly targets.

We all knew that most of these wholesalers were already loaded but he worked on the theory that overloading goods would force them to sell off excess stocks, even with additional discounts to the trade. Yet there were no complaints. The trade, he knew, valued the national prestige of working with XYZ Ceylon Ltd. because of the international stature of the holding company. And Sri Lankans have a craving for prestige.

He laid a lot of emphasis on training. Every manager had to conduct a monthly training class for his sales team, together with the monthly review meeting analysing performances against targets. These sales review meetings were held after work on the last working day of the month in the best hotel in the area, and drinks and dinner were on the company expense account. Sales people were also given company cars, with new cars replacing the old every four years. A car is a luxury and a status symbol in a developing country. Such treatment made the sales people feel that they were special, as few other companies were willing to spend so much on their staff, and their performance in turn was outstanding.

Such results do not always endear even a successful top manager to other top managers in a corporation. After some years, pressures were being applied by his fellow local directors to curb his style.

Luckily for him, his talent was recognised by the corporate head-quarters in London. The man saved himself by obtaining a new position as a sales consultant in the London offices of the holding company, a position that was far more remunerative than being a local director in a small developing country. This was primarily because local directors in developing country subsidiaries of multinationals are paid about one sixth the salary of equivalent expatriate managers, on the basis that the lifestyle of locals is cheaper than that of expatriates.

Many of us learnt a great deal about management from this extra-ordinary man. One was that ordinary employees could be pushed to exceptionally high levels of performance through the creation of happy work teams that were given recognition, better remuneration and rewards. The other was the prime importance of effective, yet highly focussed, regular performance review meetings. The third was the rewards of constant training. However, the biggest lesson was the extraordinary power that a leader could wield over subordinates by being a decent human being without the bossiness that is usually characteristic of many superiors when dealing with subordinates in developing countries.

Human behaviour cannot often be explained entirely in rational terms. External influences in the country, internal power struggles, love, hate, greed, envy and a host of emotional factors affect human conduct. Many of these differences can often be minimised by communication on a more personal level. But that is not easy if you are culturally programmed to believe that workers are an inferior class of people who should not be allowed to become too big for their boots. The workers, in turn, will resent managers who don't regard them as human beings requiring respect, despite the best public relations ploys of the Personnel Management Department.

The trade unions in XYZ Ceylon Ltd at the time were becoming increasingly restive. The salaries paid to workers in the company were by far above the national norm and working conditions were much better. But communication with the management was poor. Managers avoided direct contact with workers, mainly because their social upbringing had taught them that workers from lower classes, like the low-paid servants at home, needed to be kept in their place.

A poignant example from XYZ Ceylon Ltd illustrates this divide. Large numbers of female workers were employed in the company at the time, mainly in manual packing lines. Female supervisors were needed and the management gave these positions to socially 'well-bred' young ladies who came from middle class families and had been educated in elite secondary schools. These young women came for work rather fashionably dressed and perfumed, were treated with a lot of consideration by their senior managers and performed their supervisory tasks by elegantly parading up and down the lines of workers. They spoke and worked in English and addressed the workers in English-accented Sinhala. The workers on the lines retaliated against the perceived snobbery by loudly speculating on the physical anatomy of the supervisor in relation to her sexual behaviour, in the crudest language, with a lot of mirth and laughter, in a colloquial Sinhala language that is replete with colourful expressions for such activity. Their day would be made if they succeeded in making the supervisor run back to the manager's room in tears.

The management policy, in reaction, was to attempt to undercut the power of these unions by creating Employees' Councils that would operate separately. Every department was ordered to allocate time for employees to meet on a regular basis to discuss issues relating to their work and bring these to the notice of the Head of Department. The councils, however, had no right to discuss wages, monetary benefits or other forms of remuneration that are among the prime concerns of employees. This patent effort to emasculate workers organizations had the opposite effect. The unions made seemingly impossible demands and organized prolonged strikes to demonstrate their own power.

One consequence of these strikes was that the company could not deliver on a huge export order of 800 tons of toilet soap to a Chinese government corporation, an order that I had secured after many months of negotiations with the Commercial Secretary of the Chinese Embassy in Sri Lanka, involving numerous excellent Chinese dinners that my family enjoyed in the embassy's living quarters. Following the continuation of the strike for three months, I had to negotiate for another month to get the Chinese company to cancel the contract without penalties on the basis of *force majeure*.

Bitterness led to anger and violence. Unpopular managers were jeered by crowds of striking workers at the company gates. Two directors who went to inspect the factory were driven from the premises by a small shower of soap powder flung at them. Ultimately, the new company chairman who was sent from UK to head the company was forced to take strong measures, including the dismissal of many union activists, to gain control of the factory.

I had no involvement in union matters but I was forced into an unpleasant situation born of this conflict between management and labour. A factory worker had a deep gash on his hand and went to the company medical clinic to dress the wound. The doctor asked him how he came by his injury and he explained that he slipped and fell down in the factory and in the process cut his hand on the lid of a large metal oil drum. The senior manager in the factory later told the doctor that he had information that there was a scuffle between two workers and the man was injured. The unions had amicably settled the dispute between the two men and did not want the management to interfere.

The factory management, however, wanted to seize this issue to discredit the union and wanted an inquiry which would lead to punishments for fighting and for attempts to conceal the facts of the case. Since this was a dangerous game with a militant trade union, my director saw a wonderful opportunity and made me the inquiry officer to conduct the official inquiry to ascertain the facts of the case and recommend action. It would be a good experience for me, he said. In fact, I had conducted numerous official inquiries while working in the port and was already fully conversant with all the rules of procedure stipulated by government labour laws for such inquiries.

Thereafter, both parties sought to influence my judgement. The General Production Manager met me privately to say that it was important to punish these workers as a lesson to others who were misled by union leaders. The company medical doctor met me and said that he could prove the case for management by stating that the injury could have been made only by a sharp instrument used in an attack. At the same time, trade union leaders, who had seen management trying to influence me, sent a female employee in the supervisory grade, who was an old personal friend of mine, to contradict the management story. I remained non-committal and went about the tedious business of summoning witnesses, cross-examining them and taking down their statements in writing.

Everyone who was present in the factory at the time of the event testified that it was the result of an accident. The only contradictory statement was by the doctor. However, when I pressed the doctor, he admitted that there was the possibility of receiving such an injuring by falling against an open metal drum. It was now clear that on the basis of the available evidence there were insufficient grounds for any further action and I made my conclusions accordingly.

The moral of this story is that a harmonious workplace cannot be created out of friction. The cycle of bitterness and anger rises with each conflict. One party has to take the initiative to establish peace and cooperation. I had learnt many lessons from these incidents and will deal later with my own methods of working with unions as the CEO of a large corporation.

The importance of formal organizations to redress grievances was also forcefully brought to me by an unfortunate episode in the company. Protests by workers, consumers or businesspeople should be conducted through formal organizations with rules and discipline and should not be undertaken on an informal basis. Informal groups are sometimes organized by self-serving people to manipulate others to become the targets of hostile elements while they hide in the background and gain their ends. Beware of joining those who criticise the powers and lead you to be an outraged defender of righteous causes.

During a prolonged strike by factory workers in the company, the strikers became increasingly violent in their behaviour while picketing outside the company gates. Unpopular factory managers were first booed and then had things thrown at them while trying to cross the picket lines. I had stayed behind in the office one day after office hours to complete some work. Preparing to leave office for the day, I saw a lady supervisor in my department working late. She was known to be very unpopular with the trade union. Since the strikers were particularly restive that day, I offered to take her in my car through the workers' picket lines as I was confident of their goodwill. She declined, saying she would wait for her husband.

When I reached home, I got a telephone message that she had been physically assaulted by the strikers at the factory gates in the presence of her husband, had parts of her upper garment and her gold jewellery torn from her, and that her car had been damaged by strikers who jumped on its hood. I rushed to her house. She had returned after some hospital treatment and was in a state of shock. I advised her to report the matter to the Police. Formal agitation should not be allowed to degenerate into thuggery. That was unacceptable.

A little later she had a visit from the Vice-Chairman, who now also held the position of Personnel Director, who had already been alerted by union leaders with threats of reprisals if the matter was reported to the police. This worthy, concerned for his own safety, consoled the lady and insisted that the matter should not be taken up with the police. But she was angry and adamant and so was her family. He then offered her a singular bribe: compensation for all losses sustained and a visit to the UK at company expense for two weeks, on the pretext of training, if she dropped the police report. The offer was too tempting for a person in her humble position: it was accepted.

The violent behaviour of the strikers had now added a new dimension to the industrial dispute. The General Production Manager, a clever man in his own way, now went around to all other eight heads of departments and expressed the fear that the company would be unmanageable if the Vice-Chairman was too timid to halt the violence and the Chairman was silent on the issue. He was organizing a meeting of heads of departments to deal with the issue in his house that evening. At the meeting, he proposed that we should all address a complaint to the Chairman of XYZ International at the corporate headquarters in UK to appraise the head office of the problem in the company.

Thereafter, whisky and beer were served and the mood became frivolous. A document was drawn up which became more violent in tone with each round of drinks. It was a slanderous letter that would have only been ridiculed by the recipient. The Legal Officer and I were the only two persons who were not imbibing and were still sober. This lady and I took the document and re-wrote it as a sensible narrative to demonstrate the failure of the Vice-Chairman, in his capacity as Personnel Director, to restore discipline on account of his timidity in the face of intimidation by the union.

The next day we presented the letter to the expatriate chairman at a meeting in the board room. This gentleman was visibly frightened by a protest of all his heads of departments and tried to persuade the group to drop the matter. But many members of the group were adamant. He then asked that the complaint be delayed till he took some action. The General Production Manager, who had organized the protest, now expressed his satisfaction with this promise and there the matter ended. But the matter did not end for me. The Vice-Chairman, who was observing events from his room with concern, summoned me after the meeting. He bluntly accused me of organizing an agitation against him and being the leader of the protest. I replied that it was a group action as I did not want to implicate any others. However, he was persuaded that I was the ringleader. He retorted: 'You are the only person in that group who can write such good English. I know your style of writing. You are therefore the author of the document and the organizer of the protest'. I did not respond to this. But I had earned an eternal enmity and I knew that my prospects in the company were dimmed forever.

The General Production Manager who organized all this now became the peace-maker. Shortly afterwards, he became the Technical Director and, some years later, Vice-Chairman of the company. The moral of the story is that individuals should never be a party to agitations that are organized on an informal basis. Such agitations are usually engineered by someone for his or her own ends.

9

JUNIOR, ESCHEW THE LIMELIGHT

THE MANAGER WHO TRIES OR SEEMS TO OUTSHINE THE BOSS IS OFTEN one on his way down the ladder or out of the company. In a celebrated case, Lee Iacoca, one time Managing Director of the Ford Motor Corporation of USA, at the time the second largest corporation in the world, wrote of how he turned around his ailing company only to be dismissed by its principal owner. His case is by no means unique. Top managers are human, as human as our next-door neighbour or even any of us. If a subordinate gains too much prominence, the savage instinct of the Alpha Male in the wolf pack becomes visible in all but the wisest leaders.

There was the case of the Quality Control Manager in the company. First, he had the impudence to get a doctorate in his subject, humbling the academic qualifications of his bosses in the factory. Then he started writing and getting published in business journals and giving talks at the national Quality Control Association where he held high office as the president. Though brilliant, the man had an unprepossessing appearance: short of stature, an awkward moustache, a squeaky voice, etc. He lacked the Colombo school English accent and did not move around in the right social clubs. A whispering campaign portrayed him as a bit of a joker and a figure of fun. He was overlooked for promotion and less capable people were promoted above him. He got the message. He joined a rival manufacturing firm, a national company, as a senior director with better remuneration and presumably led a happier and more rewarding life thereafter. The vagaries of fortune will push many managers into such situations.

In 1972 Sri Lanka became a pseudo-socialist country under its new left-wing coalition government. The coalition government included the two small communist parties, one claiming allegiance to the creed of Moscow and the other to the creed of Leon Trotsky who had opposed Joseph Stalin in Russia half a century ago. While the rest of the world had forgotten these old ideological struggles among deceased Russian communists (Stalin had already been debunked by Nikita Krushchev in 1956 at the 20th Congress of the CCCP) and the largest communist party in the world was now in China led by Mao-Tsetung, who had broken with Moscow at the time, Sri Lankan communists clung to this forgotten past with a fervour.

The ageing leaders of these two parties, who had been fighting in the political arena since 1930 and made a positive contribution to Sri Lankan politics in the past, were now, at long last, cabinet ministers, holding high office in the government. They worked on their time-worn agendas. The economy was tightly closed with quotas on imports, exports and state controls on many day-to-day business activities. One stipulation was that multinational corporations that worked in the country and imported substantial quantities of raw materials from abroad must obtain export sales of non-traditional products (meaning, generally, new manufactured products rather than commodity exports) to qualify for permission to import raw material. The value of the exports entitled the exporter to Foreign Exchange Entitlement Certificates (FEECS) and only these could be used to buy US dollars or pounds sterling for import purchases or export travel.

The sudden impact of these draconian regulations caused great hardship to manufacturers. Since industry was in its infancy, there was a high dependence on imported materials. The regime of controls and permits gave obscure government officials the authority to make life and death decisions on the survival of private businesses and impacted that the lives of ordinary people. The pall of a totalitarian state descended on the country. It was a bad climate for business.

Controls stifled the country and the Gross Domestic Product declined annually. Citizens needed an official permit to travel abroad. Non-business travellers were allowed only US$15 for their entire foreign journey. Permits were needed to admit children to schools. Food coupons allowed only a limited purchase of milk powder, rice and sugar from government controlled ration stores. The owner of a rice field could not transport more than two kilos of his own rice in his vehicle without a permit while no ordinary citizen could travel with more than two kilos of rice. Private sector managers' salaries were limited to Rs 2,000 per month or about US$100. The rest was taken by the government which issued an IOU in return, cashable at some indeterminate later date or on retirement. Ownership of cultivated land was limited to 50 acres per adult person, the balance being appropriated by the state with meagre compensation. Large plantations were broken up to the point that they often became unprofitable to manage.

Big business people sat in bug-infested chairs in the dinghy corridors of the ramshackle building that housed the Ministry of Industry and Scientific Affairs to interview overbearing public officials who resented their perceived affluence and showed it. Permits were issued grudgingly, after a display of humility by the permit seekers, and received with gratitude. The prices of manufactured products were controlled, a Price Controller examining costs and arbitrarily fixing profit margins. Even a new business project required a permit, as zealous officials sought to restrict competition to prevent what was considered wasteful over-production.

XYZ Ceylon Ltd was compelled to degrade many of its reputed products due to lack of permits to import higher quality imported materials and packing. Since this affected the quality of the international brands, the headquarters in London stipulated that deviations from the product standards would not be allowed and degraded products would lose their international brand names. This affected the core competitiveness of the company. Unbeknown to the rank and file of managers, the senior directors were working hard to obtain new manufactured exports to qualify for FEECS. This was difficult, as the headquarters would not allow their subsidiary companies to export their international brands, the only products the company in Sri Lanka had experience in manufacturing. Exports were the exclusive province of the European export marketing companies of XYZ International.

Much later, perusing through a dozen thick files pertaining to export offers to overseas customers by the different directors of the company, I was amazed at their ignorance of the basics of export marketing. Export marketing was not a subject that national managers in the ex-colonies were trained in by the parent company as exports were reserved for the European companies. The net outcome was that I was unexpectedly summoned by the Acting-Chairman one day (the Chairman being on 'home leave' in the UK) and offered the post of Export Manager, a post that would be created shortly specially for me. The stipulation was that I could choose any product or group of products for export, as long as they were not registered brands of the multinational group.

It did not escape me that I, a mere Product Group Manager, was being selected for this important special post. Being somewhat wise to the trends of office politics, I was not flattered. To his amazement, I laid down drastic conditions. If I was to undertake this task, I should work on my own without the supervision of my Director with whom I had encountered many differences of opinion on management issues. He said that that was impossible in view of the organization of the company management. I replied that, in that event, I was not interested in his offer. He hesitated and then said he would consider my conditions after discussion with the Chairman who was abroad.

The next day he said he was acceding to my request, except that for the sake of formality, I would be placed in the Marketing Department in the official management chart of the company. So I became the Export Manager and through my insubordinate behaviour, earned the hostility of my supervising Director a little more.

I had visited the conglomerates large subsidiary in India a few years earlier on a management training course and studied their export operations in the Middle East, as the Indian government had earlier imposed the same requirement of export earnings that were now in force in Sri Lanka. The Indian company had successfully developed its own special cooking fat for the Middle East market. I knew that vegetable oils were cheaper in Sri Lanka, a major exporter of coconut oil, and that a Sri Lankan company could develop the product at more competitive prices. I also received some gratuitous advice from the company chairman about the potential for handicraft exports that I ignored. The handicraft business is small beer and was not likely to generate the large export earnings the company desperately needed. The company's production expertise was in soaps and cooking fats and this was the area I had in mind. They would not make investments in new business areas in the existing business climate.

This is not the place to describe the requirements for successful export marketing. Suffice it to say that I did a considerable amount of research on Middle East markets and consumers, worked for months on developing new product concepts and formulations with the very able manager who was in charge of Product Development and worked with the advertising agency on brand names and packaging. Scores of samples were first tested among the office staff and then sent to importers in the first trial market in Qatar, based on names of food importers obtained from the Qatar Chamber of Commerce. After a few weeks, there was a positive response from one big importer. The first consignment of cooking fat, described as vegetable ghee, was sent without any fanfare from the company. We had now inaugurated our own brand of cooking fats for export.

Within two weeks there was news of a disaster. The tin containers, of very poor quality and purchased from an obscure new supplier by the Buying Manager, had leaked during shipment and the goods were badly damaged and had been destroyed by the authorities in the port. If this went unrecompensed, it would be the end of our efforts in that market. I explained to the expatriate chairman that unless the entire shipment was replaced free of cost, the export effort would be over. He understood this and agreed.

The problem now was to get better packing. This was tricky as I now realized that the Buying Manager/Packaging, in partnership with the supplier, had set up a backyard plant to serve the company business. He kept insisting that this was the best available, though the tin containers were clearly substandard. They were made of low quality tin sheets soldered together by hand with lead, something not permitted in a regulated food market. Printed paper labels were then pasted on the tins in the factory. The compromise proposed by the Development Manager was to reinforce the packs by placing the cans in thick cardboard cartons that were then repacked individually in sturdy wood crates. All this involved increased costs. But this worked, barely.

With the successful acceptance of this replaced shipment, a test market was carried out in four small United Arab Emirate states (Dubai, Abu Dhabi, Sharjah, Ras-al-Kaymer) through a new importer in Dubai to test four variants of the product for brand name, pack design and product formulation. One variant proved stronger and this product and brand name was then made the standard product for the Arabian Gulf States. Thereafter, hundreds of sales letters and samples were sent to leading importers, whose names were again obtained from chambers of commerce in Afghanistan, Kuwait, Dubai, Bahrain, Abu Dhabi, Qatar, Oman, Saudi Arabia, North Yemen,[1] Djibouti and Mauritius. In the course of the next year, agencies were established in each of these countries. No doubt at all, the international prestige of the European multinational corporation helped in gaining big distributing companies as sales agents, even though we were debarred from using the corporation's European export companies' agents or their subsidiaries.

Another fortuitous circumstance was the oil price hike in the early nineteen seventies that led to a boom in the Middle East and

---

[1] Yemen was divided in the 1970s into North and South Yemen with two hostile governments. South Yemen had a 'socialist' government with rigid state controls that made business impossible while North Yemen, though less developed, had an open economy.

increased consumer spending in the region. In short order, export sales rose to US$2.0 million in the second year and reached over US$3.5 million in the third year.

My supervisor, who had initially assumed that I was on a suicidal mission with my impertinence, was alarmed. Apart from being moved to a corner of the office building, without even a full time secretary, I was now virtually an outcast. During that second year, I received a visit from this worthy at my home on the occasion of my elder son's birthday party that was being attended by his youngest son who was his classmate at school. After a scotch whisky, he sat next to me and offered some advice. 'Kenneth, this export success is a flash in the pan. It is bound to fail and that will not be good for your career. Tell the chairman that you want to move back into the marketing department and I will give you a substantially higher position.' The devil in some people does not keep quiet. I responded foolishly: 'Boss, I don't care much for promotions or higher salaries. Export marketing is a challenge and a thrill. I will take my chances.' I had cooked my goose.

Thereafter, the isolation increased and retribution followed. I was not informed of some management meetings. At production planning meetings, export production for orders in hand, based on Irrevocable Confirmed Letters of Credit, were sometimes cut on the basis that production for the local market could be affected. We lost about US$0.5 million in orders both in the 1974 and 1975 on this account and, inevitably, lost those affected importers. Exports sales volumes had to be controlled by me to avoid getting a bad name in the Middle East trade. Other colleagues went on foreign management training courses while I was ignored. Even an advertising course in Australia, approved for me by the board of directors and the UK head office, never took place as my application was mysteriously delayed and was posted after the course began. Colleagues soon sense that a man out of favour with the boss is a man to be avoided.

Support came from an unexpected quarter: the workers in the factory. I would invite foreign customers to visit the factory and introduce them to the workers and foreman on the line and praise the line workers for their devotion to export production. This made them very proud. I became some sort of hero in their eyes for creating a new market overseas where their products were appreciated.

10

THE IMPORTANCE OF NETWORKING

RECOGNITION OF PROFESSIONAL PERFORMANCE CAME FROM A TOTALLY unexpected quarter. The strength of a subsidiary of a successful multinational corporation comes from continuous oversight by the parent company's head offices, in the absence of local shareholders to supervise the board. Senior managers in the London head office who were tasked with supervising the subsidiaries in South Asia visited XYZ Ceylon Limited twice a year to evaluate performances in the areas of marketing, production and finance. They informed the export companies of XYZ International in UK and Holland of the sudden development of cooking fat export sales from a subsidiary in a remote region of the business empire. We received visits in early 1973 from the Export Director/Asia of the XYZ Export Company of UK and later, the Chairman of the XYZ Export Company of the Netherlands.

They saw an obscure manager, working from a small backroom, with one clerical assistant, getting considerable new export business by mail and telex communications without visiting any of the foreign markets. They were amazed by the results from such meagre resources and expressed their admiration of the marketing operation to the local chairman and the directors. Both men endeared themselves to me when they offered to take me in for training in their European export companies and insisted that XYZ Ceylon Ltd must allocate an annual budget for export travel and for export promotion work. They had extensive discussions with me concerning my work and the marketing techniques that had been employed. Since they ranked much higher in the corporate hierarchy than even the local chairman (rank in the international corporation went by the size of the company, not the local designation), I was now becoming a recognizable figure in the company.

They discussed what more needed to be done. In turn, I showed my gratitude by taking them on tours of the island with my family and showered them with traditional Sri Lankan hospitality with dinners at home and parties with my social contacts. Our families became friends and visited each other at home.

The next year I had a chance to visit the UK for the two training programs they arranged and the opportunity to understudy the work of key managers in both the European export companies. The project did not pass uneventfully. I was unaware of the arrangements for my visits till a week before the planned departure when the company chairman casually referred to my pending visit to the UK for training, in a conversation. I told him I was unaware of this. He was astounded that my Director had not briefed me. This was a repeat of the earlier incident of the same sort when I was informed that a planned training course in Australia was lost because my supervisor failed to make my application in time, even though it was approved several months earlier by the board of directors.

The training program was a great help as I learnt in practice what book reading, alone, cannot teach. Much of the export documentation used in Europe was brought back after the training and copied in my Sri Lankan office. I also had an export travel budget that allowed me to travel annually to Afghanistan, Kuwait, Dubai, Bahrain, Abu Dhabi, Qatar, Oman, North Yemen, Saudi Arabia, Djibouti and Mauritius (where we sold a brand of toilet soap that was designed in Sri Lanka by the export section). The business became more sustainable. Working for large multinationals has great advantages in doing business. Apart from company name recognition and the status it brings, it solves other problems. The government foreign currency controls limited funds allowed for export visits to impossibly low levels. The corporate headquarters stepped in and requested their agencies and subsidiaries in the Middle East and Africa to pick up all my expenses during export visits.

After intense internal political manoeuvring within the company, we were also able, after a few years, to persuade the top management that we should import better packaging from abroad to replace the inferior packaging the local supplier provided. This did not prove to be easy. The government officers allocating import permits had been lobbied in advance to deny this importation of packaging. The Buying Manager in charge was making all purchases of tin cans from a backyard factory in which he had a personal stake. Here, crude tin cans were made by hand-soldering cheap tinplates, while better supplies could have been obtained from a bigger and more mechanized local manufacturer. However, using my contacts with senior government officers whom I knew as students from my university days, we got licences to import cans for export products, as the only way out of the impasse.

After some time, the Buying Manager/Packaging was replaced by a new manager with a different concept of ethics, recruited from the public sector, with responsibility for imported materials. Shortly after, he received a business visit from our Hong Kong packaging supplier's Export Sales Manager. While he was meeting him to discuss import schedules, I got a call from him to join the meeting. The Hong Kong businessman had offered him 5 per cent of the value of the imports and the astonished man wanted to tell him, in my presence, that he was not open to such private commissions on company imports. Both of us urged the visitor to deduct 5 per cent from the sales price in lieu of the buyer's commission. The man from Hong Kong was equally astonished that we did not want a commission, saying that it was standard practice with the former Buying Manager.

Buyers in large corporations are faced with a trial by temptation. My experience is that they are sometimes inclined to succumb and fail the test. But windfalls also have pitfalls when they contradict the rules. A major supplier to XYZ had listed its commission payments to the Chief Buyer in its corporate accounts as business expenses.

During an audit check of the company accounts by the government Internal Revenue Department, they chanced on this and back checked to discover that the XYZ manager had not declared these takings as income. He had quite a shock when the Revenue Department phoned him and wanted immediate tax payments on this undeclared income, with the additional threat of informing his employers if it was not paid immediately.

Subsequent promotion to the position of head of the marketing department as Company Marketing Manager followed without much fanfare. The prudent manager must keep a low profile when there are few defences against hostile sniping. A section in the 1976 Report on Development in the Third World by the Chairman of XYZ International, the 10th largest corporation in the world at the time, had a rare mention of the Sri Lankan subsidiary: 'In Sri Lanka our exports rose from Rs 2 million[1] in 1971 to Rs 20 million in 1974, including notably a coconut oil-based vanaspati,[2] which we have developed for the exploding markets of the Middle East.' The compliment went without recognition within the Sri Lankan company and was never mentioned officially at any management meeting.

The company also won a National Export Award for its Middle East export marketing and the credit went to the Director who officially accepted the trophy from the Minister of Trade at the awards ceremony. The export achievement was unique in the annals of Sri Lankan business history: it was the first time that a purely Sri Lankan brand name had achieved so much success in an export market.

The benefits managers can gain by involvement in professional associations cannot be over-emphasized. During this period of Sri Lankan business history, there was considerable interest focussed on new manufactured exports. Even the government, which had only a very modest knowledge of export marketing, set

[1] These earlier exports were crude industrial by-products exported to the parent company as the local company did not have facilities for re-processing these.
[2] This is the Indian name for ghee or clarified butter.

up an Export Promotion Secretariat. The Ceylon Chamber of Commerce, the largest and most influential business chamber in the country, set up an Export Sector where I had the privilege of first being Vice-Chairman and subsequently Chairman. I went on to be elected a member of the committee of the Ceylon Chamber of Commerce, a position I continued to hold for a decade, playing a very active role in organizing new projects and thus being re-elected annually to the committee till I eventually had an illness which compelled me reduce my commitments and resign from this position.

The bigger private sector companies collaborated in 1972 to establish the Sri Lanka Institute of Marketing, of which my supervisor, who had distinguished himself in public life and was active in many social and business organizations, was the first President, an office which I took over a few years later. There were numerous seminars on marketing and business development through which I had the opportunity to become fairly well known in the country as a management expert. During the next three decades I became the most prolific speaker on marketing and management in the country. These activities gave me the exposure that allowed me to later gain popularity as a management consultant and establish my own consulting business.

The Director accompanied me for the first time on a Middle East tour of the markets in 1975 to acquaint himself of the export operation he had been kept away from for many years. His personal charm made a good impression on our overseas agents. At the end of it, we were hosted in India by one of his former Indian colleagues from the Indian company in the corporate group. Carried away perhaps after a few drinks, he boasted of his spectacular export achievements, involving arduous travel in some of the wild and remote regions of the Middle East. No mention of the Export Manager who was at his side who consequently sulked for two days.

Finally, when the Director was on long leave, the expatriate Chairman of the time called me for a personal meeting and expressed his worry that I was being sidelined in the company. He said that did not want to contradict the senior local director in his own position as a foreigner. He showed me a letter he was putting in my file saying that I was the company's choice to be the next Director, while complimenting my work achievements. This later provoked an angry confrontation with my supervisor who accused me of manipulating the chairman for my advantage. Later, he relented a little and said that I was still too young to be made a Director and that I should wait for another two years. I was 44 at the time: he was made a Director at age 39.

After a few years I realized that it was time to move away from this unhealthy corporate battleground. It is fruitless for any subordinate to continue to confront his immediate superior for such a length of time. My supervisor gave me an excellent piece of gratuitous advice when he boasted of his own success, which he believed his astrological chart had foretold, by saying: 'In my life, I have never engaged in a fight I could not win.' As in most matters, the chance to move away came from an unexpected source, without any effort on my part, because of the reputation I had built outside the company.

11

MIDDLE EAST SKETCHES: SAUDI AND YEMEN

THE PICTURE OF THE WORLD CHANGED IN 1973. AFTER THE YOM Kippur or October War, Arab nations in the Middle East embargoed oil shipments to Western countries that supported Israel. The world price of oil increased four-fold. Industrialised countries that dominated world politics were thrown into temporary recession. OPEC meetings were now at the centre of world news coverage. This rather obscure backwater of the world, with romantic visions of colourful sheiks and veiled women in harems surrounded by the desert sands and camels, became a region of prime economic and political importance for the rest of the world.

In countries where the change from obscurity and poverty to power and riches was most evident, the trend towards the insufferable arrogance of officialdom was already becoming evident, as seen in the following letters relating to my first effort to visit Saudi Arabia as an export manager. But at the same time, another wonderful human characteristic was evident. People in less industrialised, less urbanised societies lay great store by personal relations. My association with people in Yemen and Saudi, two Arab countries that were much less developed as modern societies than the Gulf States, gives an idea of the sense of brotherhood that exists among men in these societies.

At the end of 1973 I was planning my first export market tour of the Middle East after completing a six month training course with the XYZ Export companies in UK and the Netherlands. Yet managers on export tours were only allowed an exchange allowance of US$15 per day by the Sri Lankan government, barely sufficient for the tips a business traveller staying in an international hotel must pay.

It was in this repressive climate of Sri Lanka that I had agreed to become the Export Manager of XYZ Ceylon Ltd. Fortunately, XYZ International stepped in to assist the local subsidiary in Sri Lanka by agreeing to meet all my foreign travel costs such as hotel expenses, travel and sundry expenses through the offices of their local subsidiaries that were located all over the Middle East and East Africa.

While the Middle East was in the throes of changes resulting from new found affluence, Sri Lanka was in the throes of a change that was driving it towards increasing poverty. But though officialdom in the Middle East was overbearing and often ridiculous, ordinary Arabs did not lose their traditional hospitality towards strangers and my annual visits lasting around two months per year over five years from 1973 to 1977 are filled with pleasant memories.

If Ceylon was becoming a strange country during this era, the Middle East seemed even stranger as a few of my early letters from that region to my Assistant in XYZ Company, copied here, will show.

5 Granville Road
Watford, Herts
U.K.
26 September 1973

My Dear Lalith

The first lap started calamitously and didn't even get off.

You will recall that our man in Jeddah was the only agent who did not respond to our request for a visa. We wrote to Jabbir on the 4th of April and to Azizkhan on the 4th of May asking them for this (I am enclosing a copy of this as I have an extra in my file). No replies came. Jabbir then told us a visa was not necessary, it would be given to us at the airport if Azizkhan was present.

In London, I went to the Saudi Embassy at 17, Elton Place, and asked for confirmation of this. The fellow said, 'If your agent says so, do it.' This was meant to be sarcastic, but I didn't realize that. Anyway, I again wrote to Azizkhan on the 12th of September and asked him to confirm by cable that he would obtain a visa for me on arrival. No reply came to this, so I sent a reminder on the 18th September. No response still.

Meanwhile, I had sent two letters to Jabbir from here, on the 28th of August and the 8th of September on the same subject. So I confidently went to the airport on the 24th of September, only to be told that no one could board a Saudi plane to Jeddah without a prior visa. Back I went to the Saudi embassy for a visa. I was told that no visas are issued for business visits to Jeddah in London—all visas have to be obtained by local Arab agents in Jeddah and posted to London. I reminded him of what he told me previously. His response was: 'All Arab businessmen in Saudi know this rule. If your agent doesn't know his job, why should I tell you?'

I realized that if Azizkhan was not going to help, I would have to skip Jeddah and go to Yemen. So at Air Ceylon the same day I changed my ticket for departure on the 26th on the same route. I would have to stay eight hours in Jeddah airport and change over to a flight to Yemen. Air Ceylon checked with Saudi Airlines and they said that this was possible. I sent off cables to Jeddah and Yemen about altered plans the same day. However, next morning I again went to check at the Saudi Embassy. The cheeky bloody visa officer again said, 'If your airline says so, it is alright.' Back I went to the Saudi Airlines to meet the manager in person. He pulled out a rule book and showed that you need a transit visa for a stay of more than two hours. Jeddah is a special case for non-Muslims, he said.

Back I went to the Saudi embassy for a transit visa. 'It will take a few days for your visa. Nothing can be done in a hurry'. says the reprobate.

Now, very harassed and very tired, I went to the airline and asked them to re-route the journey, leaving out Saudi Arabia. The ticket to Hodeidah was made through Asmara. There is only one flight a week to Hodeidah and I had to catch that. The detour also meant that I was short of time and short of money. The ticket from Yemen back to Ethiopia would cost more and there was no time to obtain the additional money at once. I had to drop one visit on either count. Reluctantly, I decided to drop Ethiopia.

Yemen is, of course, our most important customer. The new itinerary for West Asia is given below. The programmes in the Gulf and Pakistan are unaffected.

Date	Flight	Times	Journey
1 October	ET703	19.00–04.45	London/Asmara (in transit)
2 October	IY515	10.30–12.15	Asmara/Hodeidah
7 October	IY506	09.50–11.10	Hodeidah/Aden (in transit)
7 October	DY855	14.00–15.00	Aden/Djibouti

I have sent cables and letters to all parties about the changes. So you don't have to write to any of them. I did not want to inform Hassanally of all these tedious details and cash problems so I merely referred to some problems elsewhere while making my apologies.

Show these to Mr. J and keep him fully informed.

Thank you for your letters of the 18th and 19th of September. Your note on Pakistan is very clear. I also agree with your approach to the problems with dealers in other regions. However, two general objectives must always be kept in mind and I would like you to refer to them.

Soaps

Cheap soaps (like the Russian and East German in West Asia) are sold as a commodity on price. With coconut oil, we cannot match their prices. With our toilet soap or the all-purpose soap, we can make an entry if we can establish a brand name. This demands marketing. One of my tasks is to see whether this is within our resources.

Vegetable Ghee

Though brand names are used, all the bulk packs are sold as commodities. Our present bonanza is due to the fact that many Dutch companies, including ours, are pulling out of this market as it is not very profitable in the context of high oil prices. Our competition is now coming from the inferior local brands. If we are to hold our own successfully in the long run, we must get our brand name across with a good product and good marketing. We cannot sell more and more in drums, and drums of our own peculiar size at that. We have to get into the profitable consumer packs and sell this as a branded product. Otherwise, by the time the local competitors improve, we will be out of business.

The Marketing Director will affirm that the profitable path is to up-trade the market, not to down-trade it because of local difficulties. I am off on Monday and I will send you my next note from Yemen.

With kind regards,
Sincerely,
Kenneth

PS. Revised itinerary covering Hodeidah, Asmara, Addis Ababa, Djibouti, Aden, Kuwait, Bahrain, Doha, Dubai, Muscat, Karachi and Colombo attached.

Hill-Top Hotel
Taiz, North Yemen
6 October 1973

My Dear Lalith

Yemen is a fantastic legacy of the medieval past—a primitive Oriental despotism with no coherent system of laws, no planning, no definite pattern of development. There are only two main tarred roads in this fairly vast country of 90,000 square miles and 10 million people—Hodeidah to Taiz (275 km) and Hodeidah to Sanaa (200 km). Four buses ply these roads: Hodeidah/Taiz, Taiz/Hodeidah, Hodeidah/Sanaa, Sanaa/Hodeidah. No sane man would dream of travelling in one of these buses. There are no railways. Donkey carts crowd the narrow street alleys, together with Mercedes Benz 220s. For the rest, desert trucks, camels, and donkeys.

Diseases—cholera, malaria, small-pox, leprosy, and dysentery—you name it and you have it here. The chaos, the filth, the squalor, stupidity, apathy, official corruption, these are unimaginable even by Ceylon standards. Nothing, absolutely nothing moves here without liberal doses of *baksheesh*. The main occupation is begging. Whenever the car stops to make an inquiry, hordes of determined beggars descend like locusts.

The Maashers are good businessmen, among the best in this country. They look like Pettah wholesalers, dressed in palaykat sarongs, short-sleeved shirts and slippers. They hail from Hadaramaut, in South Yemen, from where Arabs sailed and traded throughout the Indian Ocean for thousands of years in the pre-European era. The chief man in our line, Omer Mahfood Shammakh, speaks Arabic only and takes an interpreter to our meetings. But the brothers, cousins and uncles of this family run one of the biggest conglomerate business empires in the country, with offices and shops in all three main cities and in Aden: for electrical goods, motor cars, gas appliances, cosmetics, detergents and foodstuffs.

I spent two days in Hodeidah and came up to the mountains of Taiz, which is a different type of country and market, in a taxi with a driver who could barely keep the vehicle on the road at times! But more of that later: to business.

1,000 Cases White Flower Soap

I received your cable in Hodeidah. The Maashers had of course seen it as it came open through them. Since I am not seeing TRANCO, I offered it to them first. If I waited to offer it to Naiza as well, I may have missed the chance of selling it. Though the first consignment had not moved well, except in one province, they accepted it at £3.45 per case. *Please send them the pro-formas for this immediately.* Without pro-formas, you can't open an L/C or obtain an import licence. This is why the Maashers want blank pro-formas. When we send them a cabled offer, they could immediately fill the pro-formas and obtain licences and open L/Cs. We are not compromised as we act only on receipt of their L/C. Letters between Colombo and Hodeidah take 15 days in this chaotic country. In fact, in most cases our shipping documents had arrived after the arrival of the ship while the goods and consignments have mainly been cleared on guarantees.

When the L/C arrives for these 1,000 cases of White Flower, *despatch the goods by our November loader.* We must cease production of White Flower till we can review and re-formulate a new plan for laundry soap exports.

Damaged Consignment of 1,400 Cases of Ship Brand

I was ashamed for XYZ Company when I saw this consignment, partly in Hodeidah and partly in Taiz. Packing in leaky tins in polythene bags was a subterfuge unworthy of a multinational corporation and, I hope is never repeated. Also, we had not put the corrugated cardboard separators between tins and compounded the damage. What happened was that when the cases arrived in port only a few appeared damaged and the surveyors certified only these. Months later, when stocks were being issued to customers, it was found that the majority were damaged and, at this stage, they couldn't even claim insurance. I have asked them to send us a copy of their insurance claim and we must see that they get some compensation. Please don't allow such a thing to happen to any of our customers in future—it will be the end of our exports and a slur on all Ceylonese producers.

What was the condition of the balance 1,400 cases which you have just sent?

40 lb. Drums

I visited some of the backyard factories which buy our 400 lb P.I. drums. This is melted and mixed with Norwegian and Japanese fish oil, burnt native herbs (dill seed or *ulu hal* in Sinhala) and some kind of wood to make a concoction that looks like natural ghee. The factory looks like a picture out of Hades, with bare-bodied workers scurrying around huge fires in the evening light carrying firewood and drums.

I inquired in the bazaar and found that Awad M. Awad had tried to cash in on the goodwill built for our brand by the Maashers, even at a loss to himself. Our attitude to this was correct: if we allowed him to meddle in Hodeidah, he would have spoilt the market for the brand, apart from jeopardising our existing agency business. The retailers visited wanted (1) a slightly deeper orange colour for the ghee and (2) a second small outlet with a screw lid to facilitate the pouring of the liquid from the drum. Can we do this for the subsequent drum shipments?

35 lb. Tins

I have got to the bottom of this. The preference for 40 lb. tins is not one created by customers but the local Customs Dept. Duty on all tins of over 20 lbs. is assessed on the assumption that it will be 40 lbs net, if they are square tins. Since the duty is 22 per cent, importers naturally want to get 40 lbs. tins to get their money's worth. I explained our problem and said that we could have lithographed tins of Ship brand for him early if he approved the 35 lb. size. Finally, he agreed to take a small order of 150 cases of 2 × 35 lbs Ship brand in order to enable him to make a test case by protesting to the authorities (*baksheesh* will naturally be involved).

He would have to keep the consignment in the wharf for some time till the argument was concluded but since it was comparatively small he could undergo it. The terms of the agreement are as follows. (1) Consignment of 150 cases of 2 × 35 lbs. Ship brand to be sent to him by November or December. (2) Goods to be despatched by us on D/C terms (ie. Sight Draft/Cash Against Documents, through Habib Bank). (3) Strong tins, with cor-rugated board partitions between tins and no polythene bags. (4) Colour of vegetable ghee to be slightly brighter orange (ie. increase dosage of red tint in colouring). (5) The labels to have an overprint with 35 lbs (in both languages), pasted on the old 40 lbs. Please arrange the despatch of this consignment.

The Market

The market here is ideal for our level of production. Being unsophisticated and very poor, it will take our type of comparatively crude packing and production. The market leaders, way and ahead, are Telephone and Scale brands. Our product, though YR35 cheaper per case, commands much less attention. But with improved packing and a little advertising, coupled with Maashers' efforts, this is a 3,000 ton vegetable ghee market for us. More details later. The total market has not been established but I have asked Maasher to get Customs figures. It is bigger than in Saudi Arabia as the population here is bigger. The biggest sector consists of local concoctions and it is for this purpose that the drums are imported. Our P.I. is now No. 1 in drums, replacing the Norwegian and the Dutch, and at least part of this is due to Maasher's indefatigable canvassing.

Agency Agreement

After a meeting which went on till 2.00 a.m., they agreed to the text of our agency agreement with some slight modifications.

My next visit is to your friend, Awad M. Awad and also Co Harold Cie in Djibouti.

With kindest regards,
Yours sincerely,
Kenneth

New Bahauddin Hotel
New Street
Jeddah, Saudi Arabia
5 January 1974

My Dear Lalith

Arrived in Jeddah, more or less on schedule, but without any peace of mind.

I had expected to spend a quiet night in Karachi, enroute, and had not even informed our associates of my arrival. But our friends Habibi, Yamin and the banker Qasi Ahmed were on hand and took me away to one of their joints, though my hotel was booked by the airline. And a good thing too! The Saudi seat had to be re-confirmed at Karachi after some argument and, in a foreign country, these things require a willing friend with a car at his disposal.

Arriving here in Saudi Arabia was more exasperating. Travelling here is a holy punishment and no mistake about that. All passengers are checked and passed through Health, Immigration and Customs at Dhahran, the first Saudi port of call. At the Health counter a sharp, beady-eyed youngster looked at my health card for a long while and demanded a special certificate. 'What special certificate?' 'A Special Certificate to say that you are free of cholera because Ceylon is a cholera stricken country!' This was news to me. 'No certificate? Move aside!' Everyone else was passed and I was left alone. I was getting bloody worried by now. There was a doctor, Indian perhaps. I pleaded with him. He seemed to take my side. He said I would get to Jeddah. After the immigration stamp, involving more distressing rules (stamp fees £2.50, and to pay this I had to change a £20 note at 15 per cent below the official price) my passport was given to the steward of the plane for keeping. I now had visions of quarantine camps—this was what the doctor had intended. A fellow passenger confirmed that three days in a camp was not unusual.

I arrived in Jeddah thoroughly distressed and was taken to a room full of medical orderlies. The other passengers had departed. After a while, someone produced a tin of oversized pills. I was given six tablets and asked to get about my business. I was in Saudi at last.

M.U. Azizkhan is really a nice man. We had misunderstood him because he appeared before us in Colombo like a man in a mystery thriller, with his faced covered in a secretive veil. He is, however, a very affable gentleman and a clever and experienced businessman. There is some advantage in his being a commission agent and not a direct buyer. In this large market, each large wholesaler commands only a limited clientele and each wholesaler wants his own brand. Our man is therefore our salesman in a market where a resident salesman is a necessity. He is a good salesman and readily appreciated our long-term policy in the market. I will take up in brief what I propose to do.

Price

This was the most important topic. We had pushed the C&FC5 per cent price from £10.25 for the initial 4,000 cases to £10.60 for the current shipment of 1,000 cases. It would have been possible for us to push this, with some luck, above £11.00 per case, but Levers Malaysia had just circulated letters to all our chaps offering their Sun brand vegetable ghee at 10.85 C&FC5 per cent. This is clearly based on their previous palm oil prices of August, '74. They cannot possibly maintain this. I therefore settled on £10.87 C&FC5 per cent per case for December '74 bookings, up to a maximum of 2,500 cases for January/February shipment. January '75 bookings up to 2,500 cases will be at £12.50 in 1975. But we have to do our advertising and product packing development simultaneously.

Malaysia

Lever Malaysia is a brand new entry into the ghee market. I have taken Photostat copies of all their sales letters for our company discussion. We must obviously get together and formulate a common policy without price-cutting. I have seen their samples and tins. Though their pack design is unattractive, their tins are much better than ours. Anyway, we have probably forestalled them for the moment.

Tins

Whatever said and done by our buying, our tins are bloody hopeless in comparison with all others. I am sending by sea mail, two samples of tins: a) Crescent by Unilever, the premium brand, and b) a cheap Singapore brand. Both are better than ours. We have to improve our tins very fast, without being embroiled in partisan arguments and excuses. We can't get our due price till then.

Advertising

I have decided that a calendar is much better than a tin plate advertisement. The traders keep calendars; they tend to lose advertising pieces. The visual will remain the same. The calendar must be in Arabic and I will send the 1975 Arabic calendar. It will be in one sheet only. Please get working on this, consulting the MD.

Gifts

Please send one of our pen and pencil sets to each of the big buyers here by airmail: 1) Bajabir, 2) Bahasons, 3) Bamujally, 4) Al Hefni. The addresses are in our records. They present very big potential and are bigger than many of our agents.

Matron

Please get the 100 cases sample order despatched. There is a good market for a premium priced vegetable oil all-purpose soap and Matron can fit the bill. There is at present a big gap between the very expensive US/European soaps and the very cheap East European and Chinese soaps. I think that with a vegetable oil story, we can bridge the gap. More details later.

Samples

Please airmail immediately two dozen Matron and one dozen new Pears Rose to Azizkhan. There is a potential market here.

Please write to me c/o Malhotra, Kuwait. Regards to Khalid, your family and yourself.

Yours sincerely,
Kenneth

Abu Dhabi
20 December 1974

My Dear Lalith

What with the rush of trying to cover as much as possible during each short stop, interspersed with tiresome waits at airports, I haven't had the time to send you a proper letter. Today, however, is a holiday and, A&E being a work to rule subsidiary of XYZ International, manned at this point by some inhospitable South Asian expatriates, I am at a completely loose end today. Rather a dreary prospect for any commercial traveller in these antiseptic modern sheikdoms without any amenities for foreigners with sinful thoughts.

I am sending Mr J an account of my travels in West Arabia. When it goes back, please keep a typed copy for me. ....

Marketing

Marketing strategies must be worked out in detail for each of the selected markets. I have bought a copy of the Economic Intelligence Unit which gives the latest information and available statistics on the full Middle East region. We must detail out plans for sales, profits, product development work for 1975 and get it approved by the Board, and then see that these are achieved by regular Board review. I will definitely need some additional assistance to get these moving............................

Kindest regards,
Kenneth

All activity in the Middle East starts with the pious expression *Inshay Allah* or God Willing. And rightly so: the unpredictable is an ever present feature of daily life in this region. This calls for great patience on the part of any visiting business person. No patience and you will have no business in this region.

At the end of September 1973, I set off for the first destination of my first tour of the Middle East, North Yemen. The Ethiopian Airlines flight took us from London Heathrow to Asmara in Ethiopia and landed in the early hours of the next day. From there, about a dozen of us passengers were to fly to Hodeidah by Yemeni Airlines at 10.30 a.m. We waited hopefully in the tiny airport terminal. There was a small plane on the runway being repaired by a dozen bare-bodied workers in the sweltering heat. Hours passed without any announcements. By afternoon, passengers were repeatedly asking the officer at the lone airport counter for news of the departure and were re-assured with the single admonition, 'Please wait patiently.'

At around 6.00 p.m. the officer closed the counter and prepared to leave for the day. The now desperate passengers crowded him and demanded to know what was happening. 'Come tomorrow' he said. We mobbed him and insistently demanded hotel accommodation for the night. He relented and led us to some old buses which took us to a small guest house.

The next morning we arrived again at the airport terminal and waited patiently till about noon when the long awaited announcement was made to board the plane. It was then that we realized that there were dozens of other locals waiting to board the same flight, people whom we had earlier taken to be airport labourers. They rushed the plane which was soon fully loaded with big bundles of goods and cane baskets with cackling live chickens that occupied the aisles and made movement impossible. After a while, the pilot's cabin door opened and a bare-bodied sun-reddened European emerged, furiously screaming in a native language. He pushed himself down the aisle and started to throw some of the bundles and baskets out of the doorway onto the runway. He then went back to his cabin and closed the door. The passengers went out to quickly collect and reload their possessions. The air hostess then arrived. A comely dark-skinned woman in a long black dress, she ignored the passengers and walked into the pilot's cabin and locked the door behind her. We never saw her again during the journey. No doubt, she was assisting the pilot in his arduous tasks.

The plane took off like a turkey struggling to fly up. It was airborne after a while but barely skimmed the date palms and the whining of its engines indicated it was desperately trying to stay airborne. Many of the locals were either praying or counting their prayer beads. But the little plane did finally arrive at the small airport in Hodeidah, one day behind the original schedule.

I was much relieved to see our agents, the three Shammakh brothers, the senior Omer Shammakh, with Mahfood Shammakh and Mohamed Shammakh, at the foot of the stairs as I descended the plane. They had got special permission, in the usual way of the country, involving a small fee, to meet me on the runway. They seemed as happy to see me as I was to see them. They each embraced me, smacking me on each cheek with wet lips, like my old aunts would do. But there was something amiss for a fellow passenger.

In the Asmara airport lounge, I had struck up a conversation with a young English woman who was also travelling to Hodeidah alone. She was a quiet woman who told me that she had seen an advertisement in London for a nurse in a Hodeidah hospital and had secured the job through correspondence. She stood out as she was the only European woman travelling to Yemen, a region where no woman travelled without veil and a male companion.

At Hodeidah, I saw her desperately looking for someone since she was as much a stranger to the country as I was. It was now getting dark. I asked her whether we could help and she said she would be grateful if we could drop her at the hospital. I requested the Shammakhs to help her and she got into the car with us. We found the address though the Shammakhs had never heard of such a hospital. We dropped her at the site in a darkened building and left, as my hosts had no inclination to waste time on a foreign woman who was crazy enough to come without a male escort into a country where no woman ventured out on her own. I later wondered what happened to her when I came to know the country better.

Yemen, like most of the Middle East, is a male society. Throughout my visit, my agents acted as very good hosts and usually had their meals with me, either in their homes or in a restaurant. But I never saw any female members of their families who were secured away from the eyes other men. I was told that even a doctor could not attend on a female patient. A foreign doctor who operated to save a woman who was dying at childbirth was later rewarded for his good deed by being stabbed to death by her male relatives.

In this macho male society, women did not count. You could sometimes see black-hooded figures scurrying in the alleys but you never saw a woman's face. The men wore grey or green sarongs, thick belts at the waist that held them up and large curved daggers in metal scabbards. They usually wore black coats and turbans and many completed this attire by carrying an ancient rifle, much as

English country gentlemen would carry a walking stick when out-doors. Men spoke to each other so loudly and vehemently in public that you could easily have assumed that they were engaged in hostile arguments, but you would be wrong. Though people in remoter areas lived in fortified houses and shot each other over blood feuds, fisticuffs were not tolerated. Once we saw two teenage boys box each other on the streets but within a minute they were surrounded by bystanders who intervened and chased them away in different directions.

The country was gifted with three macadamised roads connect-ing the three principal towns: Hodeidah, Sanaa and Taiz, all in the habitable western region bordering the Red Sea. These were gifted by the three big powers seeking influence in the country: USA, USSR and China. The Americans and Soviets left many parts of their roads unfinished and left the country as hostile locals were shooting their engineers. The Chinese completed their road and a cemetery at the highest point on this road stands in memory of the two dozen or so Chinese engineers who fell doing their good deed for Yemen.

I visited Yemen annually from 1973 to 1978. Every time I landed in Hodeidah, the Shammakh brothers, who always referred to me as their brother, took me in their over-sized station wagon to visit Sanaa and Taiz, the other principal market-towns. I sat in the back seat with Omer Shammakh, the senior partner, with a large bundle of fresh *kat* between us. Throughout the journey, we would munch on the tender leaves and shoots of this slightly narcotic plant which put us in a mild state of euphoria. This narcotic, when consumed by the passengers, took their minds off the dangerous road which was unfinished at points, causing the car to slide dangerously, adding to the incompetence of the driver. *Kat* is widely consumed by the men in the afternoon after lunch, during this mandatory period of rest from business which opens again at about 5.00 p.m. and goes on till late in the night.

Another episode is worthy of recall because it illustrates the contradictory nature of Arab men of this region. On one occa-sion, we were travelling in the Maashers' large station wagon from

Hodeidah to Taiz, which lies near the South-Western tip of the Arabian Peninsula. It was evening but there was still plenty of daylight and we were confident we would reach the city before the town gates were closed at sunset. The scene was a picture of peace and tranquillity. On either side of the road, the desert stretched out without sign of man or beast. Suddenly, a slight black hooded figure darted across the road in front, emerging from a small group of palm-leaf shacks on the left of the road. The driver braked hard but could not avoid the creature which did not stop at the sound of the car horn. The car was stopped and we found a small slender woman who was knocked down by the side of the car but had fortunately escaped being run over.

While there was a brief discussion on how the woman could be taken for treatment to Taiz, we hardly noticed that we were being surrounded by about a dozen armed men who appeared from nowhere. They began a serious and noisy argument with us that was incomprehensible to me because it was in Arabic. After a while, it seemed settled and the woman was loaded into the luggage space behind the rear seat of the station wagon. Four of the men also got into the car with their guns, making for seven passengers plus one piece of lady luggage. We now got off the road and drove into the desert, taking instructions from our bandit companions who seemed to know their way even though there wasn't a hint of a road or pathway in the desert.

This was my first encounter with ululating Arab women. The woman in the luggage area would send out a high pitched scream that would go on for a while with a note similar to 'loo-loo-loo-loo-loo-looo-loooo', increasing in pitch with each note. She was obviously in pain and a little blood was oozing onto the rags she wore. When the noise was particularly distracting to the endless discussion in the car among its passengers, there would be a gruff command or even a cuff to dissuade the poor creature.

It was now completely dark while we travelled in the treeless desert but we eventually arrived at a small seaside town called Mocha. Mocha is a name associated with good coffee in the West but it is because this miserable little fishing port in the Red Sea was once a major export trading centre for coffee from Ethiopia and Yemen. The town was asleep when we reached a large house and knocked on its door. A Chinese man emerged. He was the doctor in the town and the house was his hospital. There was more discussion but the doctor refused to take the patient till we got police clearance. So we went off again in search of the local Police Station.

The Police Station was a large two-storied building. The Police Inspector's quarters were in an upper room. We passed a smelly room which contained a dozen goats (case evidence?) and entered a room where a small-made man was seated on a camp cot in a sparsely furnished room. He wore a green striped sarong but his upper body was bare. An old rifle hung from its sling from a large nail in the wall. A case was made and another noisy argument ensued. At one point the police officer directed his argument to me. My companions then told him that I was a visiting foreigner who did not understand Arabic. He immediately became friendly and hospitable, expressing his opinion that I looked like an Arab, but a tall one (as I was taller than all of them). He rummaged in his dusty office desk and discovered one apple. This was cleaned on the slightly soiled sarong he was wearing and offered to me as his guest. It was an offer I could not refuse. While eating the apple, tea was ordered and the atmosphere seemed more convivial. Eventually, some agreement was reached, papers and money were exchanged and we went back to the hospital to admit our patient.

Apparently, the Police Inspector drove a hard bargain on the amount of *baksheesh* due to him. At the hospital, the doctor was paid in advance and we drove back to Taiz. Once again, we had to rely on the four bandit companions for directions as there wasn't a hint of a road in the endless sands where the car would have bogged down if we strayed. The argument arose again and when it was finally settled my hosts, the Maashers, had to part with a goodly sum of money again. Nearing the main road, the bandits wanted to stop the car. Getting off the car, they prepared to leave us at last. But it was an emotional and affectionate leave taking. Each of the bandits kissed each of us on both cheeks. It was like the parting of close relatives, not of hostages taken by thieves. Both parties expressed their sadness at the parting and the bandits said something like 'Hope to see you again brothers, sometime!' This incident illustrates the quintessential Arabia, so often confusing to outsiders.

Sanaa and Taiz were medieval-style fortress towns, enclosed by high walls and ramparts and secured by enormous wooden gates at the main entrances. We were travelling to Taiz on another visit. It was getting late. We could not enter the city after sunset: the Town Guard, I was told, fired at anyone approaching the gates after this hour for fear of marauding bandits. We parked ourselves a mile outside the city gates, beside about 40 parked trucks, near a long row of tin shacks where truck drivers and the accompanying labourers slept out the night. The rooms were crowded with three-tiered metal bunks. These were nearly full and the smell of unwashed truckers was overpowering. There was no choice. I slept dressed in the business suit I was wearing: it was impossible to change clothes and I dared not bring in my suitcase from the car into this foul place.

The next morning, I needed to perform the usual morning ablutions and asked Omer Shammakh for directions to the bathrooms. He went to the doorway and extended his arm with a smile to point to the desert sands. This was the public toilet and sand was the cleaning material. I chose to wait for the hotel in the town which we would reach in a short while.

Arabs from Saudi and Yemen are embarrassingly hospitable and generous. Realizing this after my first tour, I would take ornate hand-made silver boxes, a traditional Sri Lankan handicraft, to offer to our agents at our first meeting during each visit, knowing that they would inevitably offer me expensive gifts, such as gold jewellery, on my departure, gifts that could not be refused because it would give offence to these emotional people. However, hospitality and generosity did not overshadow the Middle Eastern trait for driving a hard bargain. Knowing this, I would always ensure that price lists had an additional 10 per cent mark up to make room for bargaining. A successful bargain always gave the customer a lot of pleasure.

Omar Dahman Bamousa, one of our sales agents in Jeddah, was a different kind of Saudi businessman. He was a sprightly old man with a close cropped grey beard and a sense of humour which I could not fully enjoy as he only spoke Arabic which I was never able to master even for the simplest greetings. He was a wealthy man but money by itself was not prestigious enough in Saudi Arabia at the time: he wanted to acquire social status by being a businessman. So he began trading and was happy to import our products in large quantities, never bothering about making profits. We became friends very soon and he would take me daily to his luxurious mansion for lunch while I was in town. Before he entered the house, he would stop at the small pen near the entrance to feed the goats brought for slaughter for the next meals in the house. Goat meat was always on the luncheon menu and I found it difficult to enjoy the meat after seeing those playful creatures that we had fed.

We invited Bamousa for a holiday in Sri Lanka. After having a discussion in the offices of the company, he was leaving the building when his roving eye caught sight of the receptionist at the entrance. This lady was a former beauty queen who had been a Miss Sri Lanka at one time. Before we knew it, Bamousa had left us and was beside her, grinning and trying to proposition her in a language she could not comprehend. But he had no luck this time.

Bamousa sought my advice on getting his son into the business. I advised him to first send the boy to an American university where he could learn business management and master the English language. He accepted this and the young man entered the University of Texas from where he got an under-graduate degree and mastered enough English to send me letters on the progress of his studies and the family fortunes.

On one occasion Bamousa was intent that I should stay with him an extra week and visit Mecca with his family for the Omrah.[1] He would not take no for an answer. I would be his guest and he would buy me new travel tickets when my itinerary was changed. At length

[1] The small pilgrimage, distinct from the main pilgrimage of Haj which is seasonal.

I had to tell him, regretfully, that I was not a Muslim and could not make it: a non-Muslim visiting Mecca would face execution for polluting that holy place. He later gifted me two ornate copies of the Koran and said that one of his life's ambitions was to make me a Muslim.

Later, all our main sales agents in the Middle East were invited in turn for a holiday in Sri Lanka as guests of the XYZ Company, a gesture of hospitality that paid off very well for the business.

I like to believe that my ability to relate to the cultural mores of these societies and become personally very close to my business associates helped in developing the business we did in these countries. I was even an advisor to them on family matters as the changes in the external world were sometimes confusing to them. I discovered that the other European sales persons working in these regions did not receive the hospitality and kindness that I did. But beyond business, these were rewarding cultural experiences: eating off a common platter seated on the floor on carpets in homes, smoking a common giant hookah sitting on string beds in some city pavement, eating *kat* while travelling long distances, drinking endless glasses of sugary tea while chatting or negotiating business, and just being in the company of good friends.

12

MIDDLE EAST SKETCHES:
THE GULF AND AFGHANISTAN

THE ARABIAN GULF OR PERSIAN GULF (CHOOSE YOUR POLITICAL bias for the correct name) states were more urbanised and sophisticated because of the long British presence and successful oil production. These small states were centred round the big cities of Kuwait, Dubai, Bahrain, Abu Dhabi and Qatar, with broad roads and high-rise buildings, quite unlike the medieval fortresses of Yemen. Only Oman was different, being a large state and merely a little more advanced than Yemen at that time.

We had managed to obtain W.J. Towell & Company as the agents for XYZ Company in Kuwait and Oman. This was a prize, as W.J. Towell was the largest trading company in the Gulf at the time. Contrary to what the name would suggest, the business was owned by the Sultan family, who were Omani Arabs. The Sultan family had inherited the business from William Jack Towell, a US citizen, and his European partners, who first established the business in 1866 and then left the region, leaving the business to their Arab partner. Its prosperity was due to its management organization. Unlike the usual family owned businesses that dominated trading in the region, this company had a highly paid professional management team consisting of English educated Palestinian and Lebanese managers. The professional managerial class in the Middle East at the time consisted of mostly the American-educated and more westernised Lebanese and Palestinians, mainly graduates of the American University in Lebanon. In Kuwait, I dealt with Ali Sabri, the Kuwait Marketing Manager and a Lebanese, who handled imports.

Ali Sabri did not have the time for the intimacies and hospitality of our friends in Saudi and Yemen. However, he did have time to pick me up at the airport, make advance hotel bookings at the Sheraton Hotel and leave me again at the airport for departure from Kuwait. The Managing Partner who headed the Kuwaiti operations was Ahmed Sultan. During my visits, I would be formally introduced to him while he sat in his enormous office behind an equally enormous ornately carved desk. He was always dressed in a business suit and merely made small talk, asking me whether I was comfortable and ending by inviting me to a formal dinner. The dinners were held in a luxurious hotel dinning room of the Sheraton Hotel with the attendance of about 40 senior managers. Despite his Westernised appearance, Ahmed Sultan had not lost his cultural roots. On one occasion, I watched with amazement as a poor Arab walked into his room to pour out his tale of hardship, after which Ahmed Sultan graciously responded by opening a drawer and handing out a bundle of cash.

Ahmed Sultan had one distressing habit. He would clear his throat, then open one of his desk drawers, and spit into it. I presumed there was a spittoon hidden in the large drawer. I cannot vouch for it. Still, it seemed so out of place in these luxurious settings. His elder brother, Ali Sultan, who headed the Omani business and was the senior partner, was a different kind of person in a different kind of setting.

When I first visited Oman, in 1973, Sultan Qaboos, the new ruler, had only just overthrown his father and taken over the country. There were no big modern hotels even in Muscat and I was lodged in a large Greek guest house called Al Falaj, about 15 miles out of town, the only address for a foreign businessman but a pleasant one. It was not a picture that would have inspired many business people looking for new markets. In fact, most large Sri Lankan companies looking for the government mandated *non traditional* exports totally ignored the Middle East, which they still regarded as an economic backwater, and tried exporting handicrafts and small manufactures to the USA and UK, with only limited success. Few in Sri Lanka at the time realised the huge opportunities that were opening up in this region with the increasing demand for oil and rising oil prices.

Ali Sultan sent a car for me. He was a short rotund man, always dressed in the loose white cotton Arab costume with a white turban round his head. Muscat had poor roads and donkeys seemed to be the main form of transport for both men and goods, with a few old trucks and cars thrown in. Ali Sultan took me round the main market which was an enormous covered bazaar. The alleyways for shoppers were dug out and paved with mud and simple wood and cardboard stalls lined the alleys on either side. The whole area was covered with zinc roofing sheets and pieces of tarpaulin for, luckily, Muscat rarely witnessed rain. Muscat changed its appearance every year since then with oil money.

When I visited Muscat 12 years later on a private business visit, I was amazed to see this miserable place transformed into a modern metropolis with gleaming five star hotels, supermarkets and broad highways full of the latest luxury cars. It had also become a magnet for Sri Lankan workers. When I checked into the Inter-Continental Hotel, I was welcomed by the large Sri Lankan staff, happy to have a countryman as a guest.

The picture of the business setting in the Gulf States is not complete without a mention of the Indian merchant families from the Sindh and Gujarat who had established themselves there, as they have in almost every part of the world, and continued to live in their enclaves as though they were still in their homeland. Their success was the result of the close networks among these immigrant business families and their willingness to work very hard and endure hardships that Arabs and Europeans would rather forego.

One such business was Valabdas Muljimal & Company that obtained the agency for our products for their two branches in Bahrain and Dubai. The international prestige of XYZ International was a major factor in their wanting this agency, as big names and powerful associations are much sought after by these families that had emerged from obscurity in their own countries. Despite the many stupidities of XYZ Ceylon Limited that caused them losses on many occasions, such as late production of orders based on Irrevocable Letters of Credit, poor packaging at the commencement of the business, poor handling of shipping services, the Muljimals remained loyal to our company and continued to accept my apologies on behalf of the incompetence of our colleagues in the company.

The family maintained the cultural traditions of their village in Gujarat. The patriarch of the family was the grandfather, who had established the trading business from scratch and was now in retirement in his village in India. He had nominated two grandsons as managers of the two branches, Mahesh Muljimal in Bahrain and Lalchand Muljimal in Dubai, by-passing his own sons. I would be invited for meals at the family apartment of Mahesh in Bahrain, situated in a closed street where all the apartments belonged to Indian families who lived according to their rather frugal life-style. The women did not venture out of this street alone. I was told that there were good reasons for this. Arab men, who were used to seeing women covered from head to foot in full purdah on the streets, would become excitable at the sight of Indian women dressed in sarees revealing a goodly portion of their mid-riff and would be tempted to squeeze this area of naked flesh.

Lalchand was married around that the time and I received an invitation for the wedding ceremony in Gujarat, it being the South Asian custom to have a thousand odd wedding guests comprising all friends and associates. Though I did not attend the wedding, my supervisor and I happened to visit Dubai shortly after and we decided to wish the happy couple by visiting their home. Lalchand greeted us and invited us for dinner but the bride was missing. 'Where is your wife, Lalchand?' we asked. 'Oh, she is still in India with my mother.' 'When can we meet her?' we asked. 'She will be with my mother for at least six months? My mother will teach her how to keep house' he said apologetically. Teaching house-keeping is a euphemism for bullying by the mother-in-law who breaks the new family member by keeping her as an unpaid servant in her house till she becomes an obedient slave. It is an old Indian custom. The young woman, as she grows old and has her own sons who marry, will then get her chance to dominate the next generation of young wives.

Frugality and hard work was the characteristic of the Indian trader in the Gulf States. They worked from morning till nightfall in the business and had little recreation except for Indian films which are so popular in the region.

My recollection of our Arab business agent in Qatar is very different. This gentleman had a very large and ornate business office. He was a big handsome man with the lazy physical movements of a person who lived a relaxed and comfortable life. During one of our business meetings, a scrawny Indian man was announced. He excused himself from the discussion with me and told me he had to discuss something urgently with this man about a new maid he wanted for his house. The newcomer produced a large photo album which he showed him, standing respectfully beside his chair. While flipping through the pages of the album, my Arab associate would make these observations to the servile fellow: 'Oh, she is too dark', 'No, no, she is a little too fat', 'Her face is thin, I don't like that', 'This one is not very good looking', etc. It was 1973 and it was a first lesson on how maids are recruited for service in the Middle East.

I later had dinner with the Indian consul in Dubai who told me that he had hundreds of Indian housemaids who wanted passage back to India through the consulate because they had been physically or sexually molested by their employers. Some years later the Government of India banned the recruitment of housemaids for work in the Middle East. The Philippines and Sri Lanka then took over this miserable trade in young women who continue to be exploited for the earnings they bring back to their countries.

Afghanistan in the seventies was a different kind of country. This land stands on the ancient trade routes that connected the Western world with China and India at a time when sea routes to

Asia were unknown to Europe and, therefore, had a tumultuous past of invasions and foreign conquests. It is hard to imagine that this rigidly Islamic society was once the site of a great Buddhist civilization in the first century B.C. under the Kushan Empire and its great patron of Buddhist art and culture, Emperor Kanishka, whose name is familiar to Sri Lankan Buddhists through popular Buddhist literature.

Perhaps because Afghanistan may not have been of much interest to European multinational trading corporations, the entry of XYZ Ceylon Limited into this market with its new cooking fat and a crude all-purpose soap bar was a great success. It was a market for very basic products as the large mass of people lived with very low cash incomes. Many household consumer products at the time came to Afghanistan from the USSR and East Germany and these were of very poor quality, without brand names or any marketing. For example, the Russian bar soap was branded as '74%' and was unwrapped and smelt of crude tallow. It was no match for our soap bar, which was also unwrapped but perfumed and branded as White Flower.

Trading in Afghanistan was fraught with difficulties. Bank Melli which operated in Afghanistan was unknown to the outside world and our Financial Controller insisted on all Letters of Credit being reconfirmed by Grindlays Bank of London. Importers in Kabul also did not trust the banking system. When they wanted an import document from the bank, they brought cash in sacks from home to pay for it in advance. Goods were then shipped by exporters to the port of Karachi from where Pakistani forwarding companies sent these by rail to Peshawar. Afghan trucking companies then moved the freight from Peshawar to Kabul, Kandahar or Mazar-i-Shariff. And the market for cooking fats kept growing.

Afghanistan was an intriguing place for any traveller seeking the extraordinary. I spent around 10 days in the country during each business visit, travelling around the country with the sales agent, visiting Bamian, the great Buddhist centre with its giant Buddha statues that were later destroyed by the Taliban, the Salang Pass where a decade later Russian soldiers and the Mujahedin under Ahmed Shah Massoud fought for control of this highway to the north, the Blue Lakes, the Kabul Museum and other places of interest. The British Chairman of XYZ Ceylon Limited once queried, 'Kenneth, do you need to spend ten days in Afghanistan on each visit?' 'Yes,' I replied, 'three days for business and seven days for sight-seeing, to have an insight of the society from the perspective of a marketing man.' 'Well, I have to agree with you on that point' he responded.

The country roads out of the main cities were rough dirt roads but the lack of rain kept them in place for most of the year. The barren country looked like a wasteland without vegetation, except on either side of streams fed by the melting snows of summer, where farmers cultivated crops and fruit gardens. Herders moved their families according to the season in camel trains carrying their tents and household possessions, the women riding on horseback with their faces fully covered by coloured veils. Large mastiff-type dogs accompanied the herdsmen or guarded their tents. But the little village eating places made some of the best *naan* bread in beehive-shaped clay ovens, and the local fresh fruit was among the sweetest in the world.

The city of Kabul also had its stark contrasts. We lodged in the Inter-Continental Hotel where affluent Afghans and their families dined to background music provided by a Sri Lankan dance band while a Sri Lankan crooner sang American pop songs. Guests in lounge suits took the dance floor for a turn and drank wines, some of which were produced locally. Farther away, in the large bazaar area, the streets were full of noise and refuse and smells and customers jostled with labourers pushing handcarts in the dirty alleys. Small open shops were strung on either side of the road, filled with bulk foodstuffs and large four gallon cans of cooking fats, some of it from our company. Almost everyone here wore the loose baggy trousers with a shirt and a waistcoat, sporting turbans and full beards. The smell of the bazaar was overpowering: a combination of sweaty smells from unwashed humans, rotting garbage and the scent of spices and cheap perfumes.

The sight of so many of our cooking fats stored in a small open store with its burly bearded owner sitting cross-legged in the centre of his shop was too much for me on one occasion. I snapped a picture with the camera I always carried on such visits. Within seconds the man was on me, throttling me with his huge hands. My agent and his assistant came to my rescue and shouted to him in their language that I was a foreigner unacquainted with local customs. The man relented. He went back to his seat and insisted that I take a proper photo of him again and further insisted that I should send him a copy. I agreed and did so later when I came back to Colombo. The hospitality of the Muslim man had again surfaced.

Yet Afghanistan even at the time was a rough and dangerous country. On one visit, I planned a road trip to Kabul. I flew to Peshawar in Northern Pakistan and stayed at the Inter-Continental Hotel there. Peshawar, incidentally, was even then famed for its arms market. Guns of all sorts, from small fountain pen looking guns to rifles, were turned out in small backyard workshops and sold in the crowded bazaar areas. A partner from the sales agency, Mohamed Akram Akbar, met me at the Pakistan border post to which I took a taxi. From there, we drove by car to Kabul through the famed Khyber Pass.

The traveller immediately observes the ruggedness of the country and its people. At the small police and immigration post at the border, there was a constant stream of activity as people moved from one side of the border to the other. Most of the men ritually carried rifles and they were obliged to lean these against the garden wall before they entered the office. So the white plaster of the garden wall was always decorated with a row of guns. Once inside Afghanistan, the traveller entered a No-Man's Land of independent tribesmen before moving to the areas with government authority. Barren mountains on either side of the road revealed the occasional dwelling on a hilltop. The dwellings were small mud fortresses as blood feuds among the tribes were common. Large hoardings at points of the rough road cautioned travellers in English: 'WARNING! Do not to Stop or Alight from Vehicles'.

Another story will illustrate the rugged strength for survival that is combined with the hospitality of these people. We were travelling to Bamian and discovered towards the end of the journey that the road was closed. About two dozen vehicles lined the side of the road which was mainly a dirt track. Walking up, we discovered that a flash flood had washed away the bridge across a stream.

In any other country, this would have persuaded the vehicles to turn back and return several weeks later. But no one left. They were relaxing by their vehicles with their radios playing music. About two dozen workers were busy cutting the tall trees on the banks of the stream and carrying these manually to straddle the stream. My director, who was with me, and I doubted that they could repair the bridge with these simple efforts. But our agent was as convinced as the other travellers that the bridge would be repaired. So we retreated to the shade to spend the day in idleness. By early evening, the temporary bridge was ready. Earth and stones covered the tree trunks laid across the river and the vehicles crossed over.

Late in the evening, we were returning when someone stopped the car near the same bridge. It was the foreman of the repair gang. He wanted a lift in our vehicle as his home was on our route. We took him in and drove on. Nearing his home, he kept insisting that we should visit his home for dinner. Sadly, we declined the hospitality as we had a long way back to Kabul.

13

MULTINATIONALS ARE GOOD FOR YOU

THERE ARE INTERMINABLE ARGUMENTS ACROSS THE POLITICAL DIVIDE between free marketers and anti-globalization activists about the merits and demerits of the multinational corporations that dominate the world economy and influence its politics. But there is no gainsaying that multinational corporations are important for developing countries if only for one of the scores of other reasons: they are a valuable source of training in modern management. All the negative arguments that are brought against them notwithstanding, multinationals bring into developing countries, lost in the cocoon of bygone ages, the reality of the competitive market-driven business world that we now live in. No amount of management schooling can provide the first hand experience of successful management in competitive markets that multinationals offer its managers, especially in developing countries where lack of knowledge of modern management is the major bar to economic and business development.

Even visually, foreign multinational corporations appeared like pieces of the modern world at the time. While most government and even local private sector company offices were unkempt and chaotic, with piles of dog-eared files on dirty tables, multinational and foreign corporate offices were clean, air-conditioned and orderly. There seemed to be a sense of purpose. When I managed the State Timber

Corporation, I had to keep telling the regional managers that their offices should be painted and cleaned and that workers should be employed to maintain the gardens. Tea should be served in tea service sets and not in sloppy stained cups. Factory floors should be swept at the end of the shift. Chaotic workplaces tend to lower self-esteem and make for less productive workers.

In my subsequent work as a management consultant in Sri Lanka, and later in other developing countries and economies in transition (an expression used to describe post-communist countries striving to build market-based economies), I was constantly amazed by the lack of basic management systems even in the largest national corporations. To begin with, many of the largest and most successful corporations in Sri Lanka had no concept of corporate planning. The only plan was usually a set of financial projections prepared by the Chief Financial Officer based on an assumed (imaginary) 5 per cent or 10 per cent increase in business in each following year, a projection that had no basis and was invariably at odds with the reality of changing market conditions. To persuade managements that corporate plans must be based on research into markets, market assessments, corporate goals and objectives, and prepared on the basis of the best estimates that took into consideration both the inputs of staffs in the different company departments and the willingness of top management to make things happen to gain their declared goals through investments, training, marketing, financial restructuring, etc., was always a daunting task.

The managers in the corporate headquarters of multinationals, having worked in different markets, are usually demanding and hard on the numerous subsidiary companies that submit their future operating plans at least three or four months before the end of a year. Plans are often sent back for re-consideration of some issues that seem unrealistic or lacking in initiative. Once the plans are accepted, local managers of the subsidiaries have a large measure of freedom for operations, subject only to half-yearly visits and assessments by the head office. Major failures will result in the removal of the CEO, unobtrusively, without the local line managers being aware of what is taking place.

The importance of corporate planning and oversight in the public sector was forcefully brought to my attention a few years later. The public sector is the weakest link in the economy of a developing country. Inefficiency in the public sector drags the whole society down, not merely its economic activity. This was very true of Sri Lanka. While public sector managers are generally well educated, as the higher officers often have post-graduate degrees from prestigious universities in the West, and the majority are better educated than most private sector managers, their performance is best described as abysmal. The public sector in developing countries is usually locked into antiquated systems introduced by their former colonial masters. Since independence, many developing countries have not troubled to keep up with changes in modern management. They seem unaware that times have changed and what was relevant a century ago is now old history. They lack a focus on results, being over-concerned with the procedures laid down in old manuals of procedure.

Oversight in the public sector in Sri Lanka took a curious form. Around September each year, the line ministries would request the various departments they controlled to submit their operating expenses and capital budget requirements for the following year. Once these figures were submitted, argued over and agreed upon, these were included in the budgetary estimates of the ministry and passed to the Finance Ministry to be included in the annual national budget that is approved by parliament. Thereafter, the main concern of the ministry officials was to see whether the departments were spending their allocations. In the process, the results the public had a right to expect from such investments were hardly a consideration.

After my first year as Chairman/CEO of the State Timber Corporation, in 1980, the Minister of Lands and Land Development, the cabinet minister in charge, asked me the secret of the success of that organization. 'Why is it that only your corporation is making profits and improving business while all the others are not getting the results I want?' he asked me. My short reply was, 'Good management systems, boss. That is what I learned in the multinational corporation I worked in for 14 years. That is all there is to it.' 'Then will you teach these systems to the other heads of departments in my ministry?' 'That will not work, Sir. I am an outsider in the public service, working temporarily. I do not want to earn the hostility of the very senior men who head your important departments.' We then discussed what could be done. I proposed that the ministry hire a management consulting organization from abroad. But the minister was not very convinced. 'Westerners don't fully understand our land management systems and rural problems. Get an organization from India.'

And that is what we did. I had some contacts with the Indian Institute of Management in Ahmedabad in India from my days as President of the Sri Lanka Institute of Marketing. I went there with an Assistant Secretary in the ministry who had been appointed by the minister to oversee the management development project in the ministry. While there, we hired a consulting team consisting of three senior professors who specialized in corporate planning/marketing, land settlement/development and irrigation management. The team was headed by a highly regarded management expert, Professor Labdi Bandari. At the time, he was on the boards of 22 Indian companies. The cost of the project, which was to extend over a year, was borne by the State Timber Corporation as there was no government budgetary allocation for the project.

During the course of a year, through periodic visits, the consulting team from India conducted a series of seminars on management for top managers and then worked closely with each organization to help them prepare annual operating plans and quantified monthly achievement targets in key work areas. It was not an easy task. Changing old habits is never easy. Many senior public officials were sceptical that targets could be set for service organizations in the public sector. But it was eventually done.

The ministry created a planning department that collected all the operating plans and the monthly achievements against targets.

All departments and corporations under the ministry were required to send their monthly performances against targets to this section by the 10th day of the following month. These were then put up on large boards in the planning room and reviewed each month at a meeting presided over by the minister and attended by all heads of departments. The department and corporate heads had to explain the variances. The scheme worked very well for about six months. The young minister showed his colours as an effective manager and leader. Organizations became result conscious because failures were noted by the minister at the meetings and explanations demanded. In some cases, the minister was very severe with CEOs who had not performed. There was a sense of urgency and purpose in the departments and business corporations in the ministry.

Alas, all good things do not have a happy ending. After six months, the minister announced that he was too busy with his political work and delegated the supervision of the review meetings to the Secretary of the Ministry. The meetings then fell apart as this worthy gentleman was too gentle and was unable to exert the necessary authority over the heads of departments. After a time, the meetings were abandoned and all parties returned to their old ways. Without strong pressure on managements for performance results or self motivation, managers will seek the easy way out of problems.

This illustrates a well known management principle: management systems will only work when guided by strong leaders with a commitment to results. Without proper leadership, the best of systems will fail. But another issue needs to be addressed. Why did intelligent well meaning top managers in the public sector abandon systems that were patently better and revert to outdated work procedures? A corporate plan is only a work plan. To implement it, managers must have resources and decision-making authority. When the minister in charge presides he has the authority to approve the allocation of resources and endorse initiatives that the management proposes to implement plans. No senior official has that kind of authority in the context of developing countries like Sri Lanka where local politicians reign as petty kings and interfere with their work.

Worldwide agitation against the work of multinationals is often premised on the argument that these giant corporations simply take over the markets in developing countries and drive locals out of business. It is not an argument of left-wing agitators alone. The political campaigns against WalMart or Chinese manufacturers by their weaker rivals in the USA and their supportive local politicians, who find these arguments convenient vote garners, are on the same lines. The premise is there for all to see: in Sri Lanka, XYZ Ceylon Limited had gained 60–90 per cent of market share for many of its products. Apart from investment in modern technologies, the real secret of the success of XYZ Company was its massive investment in highly skilled marketing. National marketing was unknown in Sri Lanka till the arrival of multinationals. Multinationals sent small armies of highly trained sales people to service wholesale merchants and retail stores in every corner of the country, selling goods, putting out advertising material, displaying goods in shops, offering various promotional gimmicks. They swamped the national firms that waited for customers to come to their doorstep and spent only marginal sums on low quality advertising.

They provided important lessons for those national companies led by more enterprising local business people who were wiling to accept the new realities of business. These hired lower ranking officers from multinationals, adopted some of their marketing systems and prospered while others criticized the foreign invaders, vainly asked for protection from the state, and declined or disappeared. The paradigm is as old as civilization itself.

Modern marketing is the principal economic divide between the rich and poor countries. Multinationals, which are overwhelmingly from the major industrialized countries, do not often want to manufacture the products themselves. The most widely marketed household products today are manufactured in China or some other developing country in Asia or South America but marketed by multinationals internationally under their brand names. Even in Sri Lanka, XYZ Company contracted some local firms to manufacture some of their products which they marketed under their brand names. The practice of marketing did not reach Sri Lanka through university education. The best marketing professionals were marketing managers trained by multinationals, especially those who had also benefited from previous education at university level.

The entrance to the walled city of Taiz, in North Yemen.

The bazaar scene in Sanaa, in North Yemen.

The Kabuli shopkeeper, in Afghanistan, who wanted to throttle me.

Being received by the STC employees at the Boosa Timber Depot.

Arriving with the dignitaries at the opening of the STC forest
plantation, in Regum.

Arriving at the opening of the STC Sales Depot in Nallur, in
Jaffna District.

PUBLIC SERVICES can be MANAGED

The satisfactory administration of the country depended on the efficiency of the native chiefs and headmen, through whom all administrative acts had to be carried out....There had set in a tendency to increase unreasonably the number of these officials, all of whom had to be provided for. Bribery was largely instrumental in securing posts, and consequently it was not always that the best men were selected, while successful candidates hoped to recoup themselves for their expenditure by fleecing the villagers. The unhealthy craving for petty titles and distinctions, entailing, as it must always do, the destruction of independence and self-respect, was as strong then as it is now, and everyone connected with parties in office expected to be remembered.

—Paul E. Pieris

Ceylon and the Hollanders, 1658–1796, first published in 1918, re-published by Asian Educational Services, New Delhi, India, from the section describing the administration of the lowlands of Ceylon in the Dutch period, pages 52–53.

14

PUBLIC SERVICE MANAGEMENT

STATE POLICIES AND NATIONAL POLITICS IN SRI LANKA TOOK A dramatic turn towards a new direction in 1978 with the election of a new government advocating growth through economic liberalization. The majority in the country were disillusioned with the pseudo-socialist policies of the former government that had brought in all manner of government economic controls, nationalization of many private businesses and large commercial plantations and numerous restrictions on personal liberties, all of which contributed to a decline in living standards of ordinary citizens. State controls had been extended to every imaginable area of private business. All new investments were vetted as the government did not want new investments in areas where production capacity already existed on the grounds that competition was wasteful. All imports were subjected to permits issued by different ministries. Even private sector management salary payments had been limited to Rs 2,000 (about US $100) per month and the excess payments had to be given to the government which issued a form of promissory note redeemable on retirement.

The new government won the parliamentary elections by the largest majority the Sri Lankan legislature had seen in all its history. It liberalized the economy, attracted new local and foreign investments and undertook some very large public works with international loans, bringing in new business opportunities. The horizon for professional mangers also widened as the economy once again grew, mainly to start new businesses and find positions in the expanding private sector. Five heads of departments in the XYZ Ceylon Limited, in addition to several middle managers, left for new employment in the expanding economy. Three departmental heads, including myself, opted to join the public sector, with vastly reduced salaries, to experience the exciting prospect of participating in the development of the new economy at a senior level and escape an unhealthy management climate.

The new free-enterprise oriented government, in its initial enthusiasm, concluded that some sectors of the public service could be improved by attracting capable senior private sector managers. State-owned business enterprises in Sri Lanka, as elsewhere in South Asia, are named corporations. They are incorporated by an Act of Parliament and are within the umbrella of the ministry that is responsible for that sector of activity; the line ministry, as it is called. The Chief Executive is called the Chairman and usually combines the roles of Managing Director and Chairman of the Board and is appointed by the line minister, with the concurrence of the President of Sri Lanka.

State enterprises were notoriously inefficient in Sri Lanka, as many are even as I write. No wonder at that. The corporation chairmen and directors, with rare exceptions, are mostly a motley crowd of political appointees. They are often friends or relatives of the line minister, key unemployed party officials or parliamentarians or ministers of the ruling party who have been defeated at the polls. They are at their posts to serve the interests of the politicos of the governing party and themselves. That meant giving employment to or promoting party hacks, giving lucrative contracts to party men, donating corporate funds to dubious development funds and charities operated by cabinet ministers, securing commissions from suppliers and contractors, and all manner of malpractices that are mostly shielded from the public eye.

But not from the aggrieved employees who helplessly watched all these abuses. When a ruling government party lost power at the subsequent General Election, sensible chairmen and directors kept a wide distance from their offices and submitted their resignations to the new government, which in any case the new government would have demanded of them. The high officials who had been planted in these corporations or promoted by politicians were not so lucky. They were often physically assaulted by aggrieved employees if they turned up for work. Most of them kept away for a couple of weeks till memories faded. In egregious cases, they never returned to their workplaces.

This does not prove that Sri Lankan politicians are an exceptionally bad lot. The venality of politicians is generally universal. I can testify to this, having worked in about 35 countries, either as an export manager or an international development consultant. It is equally true of developing Third World countries and highly developed countries. And formal democratic institutions, such as multi-party elections to choose leaders, do not seem to make much of a difference. The contests for leadership often gives the advantage to the most ruthless, cunning and scheming persons as decent people everywhere hesitate to descend to such lower depths in search of political office. The difference in developing countries is that the legal checks on corrupt practice often work do not and the general population is uninformed or apathetic. The main news media are owned and controlled by the government. State organized violence against political opponents has a long tradition and its critics are intimidated.

A major obstacle to economic progress in Sri Lanka since independence has been the growing power of elected politicians who have arrogated to themselves the right to interfere in almost every facet of public administration. While there were only 50 elected officials in the legislature from 1931 to 1947, their number has increased since then to 225, making them a formidable obstruction to good management.

A few enlightened ministers in the new government made an effort to introduce better management into the public sector by recruiting senior managers from the multinational companies represented in the country. There were few takers. Public service salaries in Sri Lanka are among the lowest in the world. Add partisan politics to this and private sector managers with good salaries and secure jobs were put off.

The senior cabinet minister in the new government who was in charge of Lands & Land Development and Mahaweli[1] Development was one of the young Turks of the new government. He was considered by many as a prospective future President of Sri Lanka. A lawyer by profession, he had taken to politics at a very young age and joined one party and then another in search of political gains. He was highly focussed on his advancement in politics. Apart from this single-minded determination, he had the benefit of a clear analytical mind, an effective manner of public speaking and the ability to influence people in one-to-one meetings. He had a beguiling manner and spoke softy and gently. Most people were mesmerized when he turned on his charm and wore an angelic smile on his soft baby face. But he also had his unfathomable depths, as his associates came to see after knowing him better. He was a successful politician, and could be as ruthless as any other in seeking his ambitious goals.

I had known him socially. He invited me for discussions on national development work at his residence. The meetings usually took place in the mornings at his breakfast table where we both shared a meal. We agreed on many national issues. He then asked me to join the public sector as the Chairman/CEO of a state business enterprise, either in his ministry or in any other ministry of my choice. He mentioned that this policy of temporarily securing the services of good private sector managers to head some key state positions was the brainchild of the President himself. I had evidently been commended and strongly recommended to him by a senior director in the company and other top business people in the.

---

[1] The Mahaweli River Basin Project was the largest infrastructure project ever undertaken in Sri Lanka, involving several dams, hydro-electric power plants and new large-scale agricultural settlements.

country who knew me because of my work in the Ceylon Chamber of Commerce where I held elected office for a decade.

Despite an enthusiasm for development work, I had several reservations, knowing well that public sector business corporations were highly politicized. Senior public service salaries were very low compared to what I received at XYZ Ceylon Ltd. He then appealed to my patriotism, arguing that we should all sacrifice a few years of our lives to rebuild the country for the next generation. He also promised me that he would not allow any politician to interfere in my work if I joined his ministry. He assured me, 'You will have the authority to run a substantial business like your own private company.' The opportunity to run a business as CEO was too much of a temptation. I chose to be Chairman/CEO of the State Timber Corporation (usually referred to as the STC), one of the two business enterprises in his ministry, because it seemingly had the biggest problems but was also a good prospect for a business turnaround. I would initially take two years leave of absence from the company and take this position.

The STC was a large organization with around 2,100 employees and had the sole monopoly for the extraction and sale of all timber from the state forests of the country. The large areas of national forests and state forest plantations were managed for the state by the Forest Department. The STC managed harvesting and marketing of forest products on a monopoly basis, depending on the forest allocations made to it by the Forest Department, paying 10 per cent as royalty to the government for the privilege. The STC also had its workshops and large sawmills where logs were sawn and others were converted into railway sleepers and transmission poles. Despite this monopoly of harvesting state forests, the STC had never made profits in the decade of its existence. It presented an exciting opportunity for any ambitious manager.

With the letter of appointment from the government in my pocket, I went with my wife to visit my supervising Director to request him for a couple of years of leave of absence from the company, certain that he would be glad to see the back of a disagreeable subordinate.

Imagine our astonishment when he burst out angrily and told me that I would not be permitted to leave as I was 'the only trained senior marketing manager in the company'. We went away confused. The next day I checked with the Chairman who said he would be willing to comply with my request, provided I managed to persuade my supervisor. A strongly worded personal letter from the Minister of Lands & Land Development to the Chairman of the company, expressing the dissatisfaction of the government with his attitude, settled this issue and paved the way for two years of leave of absence without pay from the company.

But I hesitate to be ungenerous to my former supervisor. A few years later, when the STC's high performance under my management became the subject of considerable media exposure, he sent me a glowing letter of congratulation stating that he knew that those managers trained by him would go on to do greater things.

Meanwhile, I had a visit at home from a senior employee of the STC whom I knew personally. This person told me that the STC was a difficult place to reform and that all previous attempts to improve it had failed, despite the best efforts of capable men. There was a lot of friction between the top management and the employees. The previous Chairman, whose position had not been filled for several months since his departure, had suffered the indignity of being physically assaulted by the STC employees at the Minneriya sawmill complex that caused him to leave the corporation in disgrace.

The former Chairman had gone there after a severe cyclone had devastated the Eastern Province in 1978 to inspect the damage to the corporation and the surrounding teak plantations. He was soon surrounded by STC employees and their families who came to him seeking urgent assistance as the cyclone had damaged their homes and caused them severe personal hardship. The Chairman, who in previous employment had been a tea planter and was more familiar with the humbler tea plantation labour, addressed them rudely and refused to be concerned with their personal woes. The enraged employees then set upon him with fists, forcing him to take refuge in an office where he locked himself for protection. He was finally rescued by an armed police party that his chauffeur had the sense to contact as the motor car he came in had been parked outside the main gate. In a subsequent court case, four employees were jailed for assaulting the chairman and a dozen others dismissed from the service of the STC. My friend's sincere advice to me was that I should remain in XYZ Company where he felt I was much better off.

Further information on the management of the STC was gleaned from this officer. The efforts to reform the STC in the recent past were, I was told, based on a number of new rules applied to employees to improve discipline. The management of the corporation was in large part in the hands of the General Manager. This worthy gentleman, a very experienced forester with solid academic qualifications, and a hardworking man of great personal integrity, was in the mould of the old-school headmaster who followed the adage of 'spare the rod and spoil the child'. A big man of stern appearance, he guided the previous Chairman who was lost in the new environment of the STC which seemed so different from the tea plantations he had managed.

Every month, the duo would undertake a tour of a few of the 40 odd offices and 200 work points of the STC and look for infractions of the rules by employees. They would successfully return with several cases of misconduct and issue 'show cause' notices to the errant employees that ultimately led to punishments ranging from fines to dismissal. This had built up hostility against the General Manager and the Chairman, and the top management in general. After the change of government with the recent General Election, employees had planned to use this excuse to assault the General Manager (who had no political affiliations, to begin with) who wisely kept away from his office for two weeks till tempers cooled.

Meanwhile, the entire board of directors of the STC was changed by the minister. The new appointees, with one exception, were reasonably good men by public sector standards. The Working Director, Mr Wettewe, though a cousin of the minister, was a lawyer and a man of immense goodwill and decency. Another was the Conservator of Forests, who held the post ex-officio. Another director was a provincial lawyer with close political affiliations to the minister. The fourth person was a minor local political hustler of the governing party from Moratuwa, a town to the south of Colombo which was the heart of the furniture industry in the country. Since this town was the major user of luxury timbers, the Member of Parliament for the area was traditionally allowed to propose someone for the board of the STC. In this case, the person's credentials aroused some doubts in my mind though I felt I could manage him with some goodwill gestures.

At the very first meeting of the new board of directors of the STC, I sought a commitment from my fellow directors. 'Gentlemen, we are here together as a group of honourable men, dedicated to creating a better business out of the State Timber Corporation. We have much work to do but it will never be done if we work for our own private ends. So let us make an undertaking that we will not seek any personal advantages for ourselves or our friends from this business. For my part, I assure you that I will not appoint any of my relatives or friends to the STC or favour them through other means. I know you will join me in such an undertaking.'

There was a chorus of 'Yes, yes.' I knew that this would make it impossible for any of them to come to me for special favours in future. Whatever they may want to manipulate for themselves, they would now have to do it without my knowledge.

15

MEETING THE PEOPLE

I WAS STILL IN MY OFFICE IN THE XYZ COMPANY AT THE BEGINNING of 1979 completing my pending work before departure, when I received a visit from the new working director of the STC. He addressed me very formally: 'Mr Chairman, we need to work on the new private sector management systems that you will decide to bring into the STC when we start work shortly. The Honourable Minister wants us to start work with the new board of directors very soon.'

He was a kindly middle-aged man whom I came to respect very much when I got to know him better. His knowledge of management did not amount to much at the time but he was determined to learn and regarded me with some awe as a guru in management on the basis of my reputation in business circles in the country. I responded that we had to face a bigger hurdle before we started work. The employees of the STC were hostile to the management. We had to gain acceptance within the organization if any of our reforms were to be effective. I told him that his experience in politics would help us in this work, the details of which I was working on.

I also received a visit from the General Manager of the STC at my residence. He urged me to come to office soon as a considerable amount of work awaited the instructions of the new Chairman. In the absence of a Chairman for over three months, the corporation was

unable to carry out certain work programs. This information mysti-
fied me at the time but I promised him that I would arrive at my
desk in another month.

Having said my farewell to my friends in the company, I duly
arrived at my desk in the STC without any fanfare. The Chairman's
official car and driver arrived at my house to convey me to the office.
I was met by the General Manager who took me to the chairman's
seedy little office where a large table was piled high with about 40
bulky dog-eared files. He told me these were awaiting the chairman's
signature. I looked into a file and could make no sense of their import.
I asked him what they were. They were requests for overtime allocations for employees from 40 different offices. I asked him why they
had come to me. He answered: 'Overtime is directly authorized only
by the chairman to prevent abuse and excessive demands. This is
also a measure to reduce costs. Without your signature, some work
will continue to be held up.' It occurred to me that the signature of
the chairman, who had no idea of the workload at the work points,
seemed meaningless. I merely replied: 'Send it back to the managers
at the work points and let them decide. I will not sign any overtime
applications while I am here.'

This response caused consternation. The General Manager was
incredulous. 'You will not sign these overtime applications?' he asked
again. I said firmly, 'I have already told you. I will not sign any overtime approvals while I am here. That is a decision for the manager at
the site.' He was unhappily becoming aware that the new chairman
would not be his willing pupil.

Shortly after, together with the Working Director, I summoned
a meeting of all the senior managers. At the meeting, I introduced
myself and the new Working Director and expressed the usual cordial
greetings to those present. I told the meeting that both of us were
new to the business and needed to know more about it before
starting work. The first questions went as follows.

'Give us an idea of this business. What is the market that the
STC is working in? Who are the consumers? What is the size of the
total market for timber in the country? What is the market share
of the STC? Who are your main competitors?'

There was a long silence. The General Manager, perhaps with the notion of putting these would-be reformers in their place, then spoke up: 'We have no idea what you are talking about, Sir. By the Government's Act of Incorporation, we have the monopoly of the extraction of timber from state forests. These are allocated for felling by the Forest Department. We fell the timber and sell it, as logs or in processed form, on the basis of allocations given in permits. That is the work of this corporation.' That ended the meeting. It was evident that there was a lot of work to be done to give some direction to a management that did not know what their business was and where the business was going.

The next day we commenced the public relations campaign. The Working Director and I arrived early at the Accounts Department which was housed in a large building about three miles away from the head office. We went first to the office of the Chief Accountant, greeted him and introduced ourselves. We then requested him to take us to the cubicles of the other officers. We greeted each officer personally, inquired about their work and exchanged a few pleasantries. We then walked up to the desks of each of the 80 odd employees in the office, mostly clerks and typists, greeted each one of them personally, shook hands with them, and asked them for their names and the work they performed. Finally, we looked for the *peons* in the office, those indispensable office labourers that do the odd jobs in every office and are looked upon with disdain by their superiors, and shook hands with each of them and greeted them cordially.

There was now an element of consternation and disbelief. I was later told that no chairman had ever greeted employees in this manner in the history of the public service, certainly not lowly peons. After these greetings, I requested all the employees in the office to stop work and gather round the main office area for a meeting. Then I addressed them on the following lines.

'On behalf of the new board of directors of the STC, I want to introduce ourselves to you and share our vision for the STC. The new Working Director and I are here on an assignment for a few years to work with you to improve this business. Let me tell you from the start that we are not here to enrich ourselves personally or play partisan politics. I have temporarily given up a lucrative job in a multi-national corporation and I do not propose to stay here for more than two or three years. Mr Wettewe has given up a legal practice to become your Working Director.'

'We sincerely believe that this corporation has tremendous potential for growth and profitability which have still to be developed. We can do this together and make this a substantial business that will be of benefit to the general public that wants timber products; the government, which as the owner of the business, will receive more revenue; and you, as employees, who will obtain much better benefits and working conditions.'

'We assure you that we do not seek any such benefits for ourselves personally. We look forward to working with you in a spirit of co-operation and goodwill.'

A speech from the Working Director in a similar vein and a message of thanks from the Chief Accountant followed. At the end of the meeting, we were aware that we had created the kind of friendly atmosphere that had never existed before. We were later told that some employees had stated that they never expected to see the day when the Chairman would shake hands with them because chairmen usually walked past employees with their heads in the sky.

This type of meeting was replicated in some other big worksites around Colombo with equal success. We did not need to go everywhere in the country on this goodwill tour, as the word had quickly spread through the corporation and we now needed to start work to implement our vision. But we were painfully aware that unless we made good on our promises very soon, the employees would take us for another group of slick talkers who, like most politicians, made empty promises.

Winning goodwill was the key issue but establishing authority was another. We sensed the subtle efforts of the General Manager to belittle the new chairman who was planning revolutionary changes without seeking his guidance as past chairmen had done. He was older than me and had privately expressed the view that a person without experience of forestry would not be competent to lead the STC. At the first meeting of the new board of directors, I was addressing the meeting from the chair when I noticed that the General Manager, who was customarily invited to be present, was talking to his immediate neighbour without listening to me. I stopped speaking and hit the table violently with my fist. When there was the expected stunned silence, I exploded: 'Will you shut up, Mr R, and follow the meeting! If you have any questions, you will address the chair. That is common courtesy. If you are not interested in the proceedings, kindly leave this room.' Mr R, astounded by this outburst, bowed his head and kept quiet.

I knew that news of this public humiliation of the big man would spread through the STC. People would know that the unpopular GM had been put in his place. They would realise that the new chairman was kind but could not be trifled with. It was a good starting point.

16

MAKING A QUICK BUCK

RESPONSE TO THE FIRST MANAGEMENT REFORM IN THE STC WAS dramatic. One morning, a month after assuming office, there was a commotion down the street where the chairman's office was located. There were scores of rough characters in an angry mood marching towards the office and some of them were shouting slogans against me. At their head walked the Junior Cabinet Minister for Foreign Affairs and Member of Parliament for Moratuwa, a town south of Colombo that was the centre of the carpentry industry in Sri Lanka. This worthy smiled apologetically and entered my office. He was a portly gentleman who hailed from a prominent Sri Lankan family and had attended the same secondary school that I did as a young student before he went to Oxford University in England for higher studies. It seemed incongruous that a member of the social elite should lead such a rabble. I told him that for the sake of good order and discipline, all his raucous supporters should stay outside the office premises.

Soon after assuming office, we had studied the Profit & Loss Accounts and Balance Sheets of the corporation and discussed these with the Chief Accountant and the Chief Operations Manager. The reason for the very low sales turnover of the STC, around Rs 58 million the previous year, was soon apparent. The STC sold the bulk of its luxury timber through about 250 'Registered Direct Users'. These people, they said, were political beneficiaries of the government.

They were supporters of the ruling party who had no real business except that they obtained a Direct User Permit from the STC for a large quantity of luxury timber which they then sold to genuine manufacturers, sometimes for as much as half a million rupees or more. Genuine manufacturers and house-builders were usually unable to obtain timber, all of which was given only on permits, without some influence through politicians or state officials. As a result, the STC sold the timber at a very low price, below the real cost of production, while the market price for the same timber was about three times higher.

No one in the STC had previously dared to bell the political cat. It was now time to do so and test my real authority based on the undertaking given by my minister. I spoke to the officials in the ministry and said I wanted a group of senior officers to carry out an independent survey of the Direct User manufacturers who were receiving special timber supplies on permits. The ministry allocated a senior officer who had at one time been a Senior Superintendent of Police to lead the team of investigators. I then prepared a letter that was sent by registered post to all the Registered Direct Users. I stated, tongue in cheek, that we had decided to improve allocations to permit holders and that the volumes of future timber issues would be determined after a survey of each workplace by the ministry officials. The ministry officials would want to see their business registration, the last tax payments made by their business, the manufacturing facilities, the number of employees and the last audited accounts.

The results were more surprising than we expected. More than two hundred letters were returned by the post office with the stamped remark, 'Addressee Unkown'. None of the others responded to our letter. We then took the next logical step and cancelled all the permits. And this was the cause of the mob rally against me. The dice was cast.

I innocently asked the minister what the commotion was all about. He responded: 'I say, Mr. Chairman. You have caused a lot of trouble by cancelling all the Direct User permits. These people are mainly my constituents. You can't do this to them.'

I stated: 'Sir, you know as well as I do that these people are frauds. They are not direct users. They make a good living by selling the timber permits to genuine users. We can't allow that and run this corporation properly.'

'That is true. But they are our staunch political supporters. We have to look after them.' I responded, 'That is your problem, Sir, not mine. I will not allow it. You may have heard that I came from a good position in a large multinational corporation at the request of your government. My job is to reform this business. If you don't like my attitude, I am willing to go up to the President of Sri Lanka over this matter and even resign from this place.'

'No, no. We don't want to take it so far. But can you make some accommodation?' I replied firmly, 'I am sorry, Sir. I cannot.'

There the matter ended. I don't know what he told his supporters and what other promises were made to them but they went away peacefully from the scene. There were some incidents later where some of these thugs tried to harass the local STC officers and inter-rupt its business in Moratuwa. When the STC opened a new sales depot near Moratuwa to serve the genuine industrial users in this carpentry town, these thugs attacked the trucks of customers on the road to the sales depot. But these were minor irritations. The hire of security services managed by a former Deputy Inspector-General of Police solved that problem. But a major victory was achieved. It was now possible to supply the needs of the actual users through a liberal sales policy. This was not difficult. The names of the large furniture manufacturers and other timber users were well known to the STC as well as the public.

Sales picked up but there was another major hurdle. Since the STC sales prices were far less than the market prices and high quality furniture timber, mainly teak, mahogany and satinwood, were in short supply, prices needed to be adjusted upwards to match something closer to the prevailing market prices. The prevailing prices did not cover operating costs. Price adjustments were blocked by another political obstacle. The managers informed me that the previous Chairman had tried to increase prices but that an influential businessman, a friend of the President of the country, who owned an export-oriented parquet flooring business based on STC timber supplies, had taken the matter up with the President of Sri Lanka who personally ordered the Chairman of the STC to withdraw the price increases. The same gentleman would object to any price increases and use his influence with the President again.

The solution to this obstacle had to be different. I knew the gentleman who headed this parquet business socially. His major purchase was teak *thinnings*. Thinnings are immature teak trees that are thinned out in rows from teak plantations to allow the remaining trees room for growth. Apart from the STC that used a part of these for conversion to transmission poles, the parquet business was the only other major customer for thinnings. I informed this gentleman that I was increasing all timber prices, with the exception of teak thinnings, purely for his benefit. I wanted his assurance that he would not raise objections to the general price increase at higher quarters. He agreed to this arrangement. Thereafter, the new price list was published. Prices were doubled on average but were still about a third less than prevailing open market prices. Within the month, the STC was registering profits.

The third major obstacle to sales was the lack of adequate supplies for the STC. The demand for timber was rising with the huge investments in construction that were taking place as a result of the new government's open market policies. The available local forest resources were limited. The supplies available to the STC were also curtailed by a strange bureaucratic obstacle, typical of the strange devices that only bureaucrats can dream up.

The harvesting of timber in about 200 felling areas was done by private contractors hired by the STC. Most of these contractors had been in the business for many decades, for work in the remote forest areas of the country required special skills and resources, as well as endurance of difficult living conditions. Their task was to fell mature trees selectively marked for felling by the Forest Department in the natural forests. In plantations forests, they carried out clear felling of all trees in a given area to allow for replanting afterwards. These felled logs were then were stamped by STC supervisors for identification and transported to the STC timber sales depots. Each log was then assessed for its value and the contractor was paid a fee based on the logs supplied.

Costs had gone up considerably over the last years, especially because the new open economy had fuelled inflation, but the STC could not pay the contractors to cover their costs as the STC selling prices had been kept artificially low, up to now. So the STC had come up with a new device. The contractors were paid a low fee that did not cover their costs. To make up for this, contractors were allowed to take away a proportion of the felled timber for direct sale by themselves. To justify this concession, the logs taken by the contractors were classified as 'unwanted timber'. These logs were also stamped by the STC as only the logs bearing an STC stamp could be transported on the main roads from the forests.

This strange bargain led to a decline in supplies to the STC. Contractors naturally took a substantial portion of the best logs for their own sales while deliveries to the STC declined. Since contractors did not pay for the logs, they made very substantial profits from this scheme by marketing timber on their own. After the successful price increase, the STC informed the contractors that it proposed to increase the contract fees but needed information on their costs of production. The contractors were at first unwilling to change the status quo which was profitable for them. But after holding several meetings with the contractors to seek their point of view, costs were obtained from a few big contractors, analysed by the accountants and new contract fees were announced. These were substantially higher than the old fees and allowed for a good profit margin and the 'unwanted timber' extraction was stopped forthwith.

With these changes, the STC sales figures climbed in a manner that surprised even the STC management. By the sixth month, the STC was making substantial profits. It was now time to redeem some of the promises made by us to the STC employees.

Two other fortuitous circumstances came up to assist the STC to increase its production and sales. Large areas of teak forest plantations belonging to the Forest Department had been felled by a cyclone in the Eastern Province in 1978 but these trees had not been harvested by the STC because of sheer inertia and lack of planning. It was now becoming a fire hazard in the dry season. A special project to harvest this teak expeditiously brought in a huge stock of luxury timber that would provide a bonanza for a few years.

The other windfall was the decision of the government to clear around 600,000 acres of forest land, much of it denuded secondary forests in the Eastern Province, under the Mahaweli land settlement scheme. The job had to be done within a tight time schedule as the settlers would be brought in as soon as a series of reservoirs were completed on the Mahaweli River. The story of how this was done is found in the subsequent chapter.

Despite the increase in supplies, sales and customer services lagged behind. Government business enterprises in Sri Lanka operate on the basis that they do the customers a big favour by selling their goods. Customers are made to wait while employees engage in other tasks and cumbersome sales procedures delay the purchases. The existing sales network was also insufficient to handle the increasing volumes. The new government had come into power with a philosophy of an open market economy and it was reasonable to bring in private sales depots which would operate like STC franchises. Gaps in the sales network were identified and new sales depots were opened, both as STC depots and STC franchises.

This also allowed for a relaxation of the permit system for the purchase of teak by genuine house-builders. Permit systems inevitably cause corruption. When I was building a house for myself in 1974, five years before I came to the STC, my request for a permit to buy 25 cubic feet of teak was rejected by the STC. One of my assistants at XYZ Company then obtained it for me through the intervention of the Secretary to the then Chairman, who was his cousin. I ended up buying the rest of the timbers for this fairly large house from a private timber dealership north of Colombo. The service here was exceptional. When my wife hesitated to buy all the timber requirements in one lot due to cash constraints, the proprietor told her that he knew that I worked as a top manager at XYZ Company and she could have all her requirements on credit. Later, when I was Chairman of STC, this same gentleman came to me for a special favour which I could not allow him. I would later tell this to the STC managers to stress the need to eliminate permits and provide a service to consumers. Government officials tend to love permit systems: it makes even humble officers seem very important.

17

REDEEMING PROMISES

THE TIME WAS NOW RIGHT TO REDEEM THE PROMISE TO THE employees by improving their existing conditions of work. Substantial benefits, given six months after the new Board of Directors took office, would have a strong impact on the employees' morale and their opinion of the new management. It was proposed to the Board of Directors that all employee salaries should be increased, except that of the Working Director and Chairman, by a minimum of 30 per cent. But the quantum of increase for each category of employee would be decided by a job evaluation carried out by a reputed government management development organization, the National Institute of Business Management (NIBM). To gain acceptance for this proposition of different levels of salary increases, which could be confusing to some employees, all office-bearers of the seven trade unions in the STC were first made to participate in a week-long training course at the NIBM, to become versed in the rationale and mechanics of job evaluation.

At the conclusion of the job evaluation, the very next month, the salary increases were announced. The quantum of the salary increase took the trade unions quite by surprise. Traditionally, benefits and salary increases came only after trade union agitation and negotiations with management. It was quite unusual for a management to take the initiative without any prompting from the unions.

Relations with the unions needed redefinition. There were seven trade unions, each one owing allegiance to a political party in the country. However, the union affiliated to the ruling government party always felt that they had the ear of the directors and had special privileges. In some government corporations, the prevailing government trade union, known by the acronym JSS, had its own offices allocated by the management within the business premises and trade union officials dictated to the managements on some key issues. Soon after our taking office, the officials of this union met us and wanted to have a special meeting with the top management. I declined the request and made it clear that the management would only meet with all the seven unions at any given time. The timely award of higher salaries made it impossible for these union leaders who felt neglected to persuade their members to criticise the new management.

Another worry that faced employees was the dread of being transferred to work in the Mahaweli Development Area. The Mahaweli River Basin Development Program was the largest infrastructure development program undertaken in the history of the country in modern times. It was funded by the World Bank along with several bi-lateral aid agencies and cost over US$ 2 billion at the time. The largest river in the country was to be dammed at several points to provide hydro-power and water for the irrigation of about 650,000 acres of land in the North Eastern Dry Zone of the country. This was a part of the traditional homeland of the ancient Sri Lankans, now long abandoned for over a thousand years due to South Indian invasions and the destruction of the ancient irrigation systems that supported rice cultivation. Now the government planned to settle about 200,000 landless families in this region which had become a vast area of denuded secondary forest. The task of forest clearance and the building of the initial forest roads was the job of the STC.

STC employees, quite naturally, were unwilling leave their settled places of residence to re-locate in jungle areas where living conditions were harsh and very primitive. As a result, there was a lot of discontent. Employees who were transferred to this location refused to take up work in the area and tried to obtain relief by producing bogus medical certificates or letters of support from Members of Parliament seeking exemption. More important, work on jungle clearing and the preparation of land for settlements was already far behind schedule. The Chairman of the Mahaweli Board, who was also the Chairman of the ruling government political party and a very abrasive character, was often on the phone, criticizing me for the slow pace of work by the STC. This irascible character was so powerful that even our minister and the Secretary of the Ministry left him alone and stayed out of his way.

The other constraint was that the traditional methods of forest felling used by STC contractors, using axes for felling trees and elephants to carry them out, were unsuitable for quick clear-felling of large areas of land. Elephants were ideal for dragging out felled trees that had been tagged by the Forest Department where selective felling was the norm in natural forests. Here, there were perhaps no more than five trees per acre to be felled. Elephants, being the formidable creatures of these forests, eliminated the need for forest roads to every tree that was felled and made the operation of felling a few trees per acre of forest profitable. But there was a need for mechanized jungle clearance in the Mahaweli area if all trees and scrub were to be removed expeditiously.

The first problem of persuading employees to relocate was done by using simple common sense, that rare gift that often eludes public sector managements. I told the top management who seemed helpless on the matter that people are persuaded when benefits outweigh the inconveniences. Accordingly, all personnel working in the Mahaweli area were given a special living allowance, in addition to pay, ranging upwards from a minimum of Rs 1,750 for the lowest category of employees. The STC would also have a program to urgently build temporary housing for employees working in the Mahaweli area. The increased costs would be covered by the increased volumes of timber that would be harvested from the Mahaweli jungles in a shorter period of time. The incentive scheme worked better than anticipated. There was now a demand for work in the Mahaweli that exceeded the work requirements.

The second problem of mechanization was easily solved by the purchase of large forest clearing machines, called timber jacks, big log transport trucks, dozers, chain saws and other machinery and equipment. The proposal for this capital investment, all of it to be funded from the newly available internal resources of the STC, without bank borrowing or the usual request for government supplementary allocations, was still to face some hurdles. The Ministry of Finance and its External Resources Department had many questions about the investment. I interviewed the senior government officers concerned. After perusing the documents, they expressed their misgivings about the financial projections. Their fears were justified. 'We have seen nice proposals like this on paper before,' one senior officer remarked, 'but they never work out in practice in a government organisation.' I concurred. I said that this time the implementation would be the responsibility of a private sector manager, myself. I told him that I took full responsibility for the results. I alone, as the Chief Executive, was the guarantee of the success of the project. This brash and egotistic answer seemed to be convincing enough to him and the project was approved.

My encounter with the Secretary to the Treasury of the time to receive the final approvals must be related. This top civil servant was a very personable man, handsome and debonair, much sought after in high social circles in Colombo by top business people. When I was ushered into his large expensively furnished office in the Treasury building, he waved me to seat myself in one of the luxurious sofas at the other end of the room. He excused himself and continued with his work for about 10 minutes, scanning and signing documents. After finishing that task, he leaned back in his revolving chair and opened a drawer, took out a pack of cigarettes and put one on his lips. An adjoining door opened instantly and a male secretary rushed up with a cigarette lighter and lit his cigarette and went back. He then beckoned me to start the meeting. Such colourful aristocrats still existed in the upper echelons of the public service.

Work in the Mahaweli Development Project provided a window into the technological achievements of the ancient Sri Lankans and the great civilization they had created around two millennia ago. Consulting engineers from the Canadian International Development Agency carried out sophisticated surveys to identify the most suitable site for the 40 meter high dam across the Maduru Oya River. Clearing the thick jungle at this place revealed the remains of an ancient irrigation bund, 27 meters high with two sluice gates and conduits for upstream water control. We were all amazed. The Canadian consultants sent the following report to our Minister on the discovery.

'The upstream portion of the sluice is a masterpiece of construction. Twin conduits with corbelled arches approximately 2.5 meters apart pass through the bund. At the downstream is a carved terracotta relief depositing between the two arches. The dancing figures have been mutilated and the marks of the chisel used can be clearly seen on the carved relief.

'Major irrigation works and water control structures have been constructed throughout the civilized world since the 4th Millenium B.C. These works include earth and rock dams, spillways, canals, dykes and embankments—the same structures that modern day engineers design for the same purposes. Some of the structures were advanced in engineering concept, major in scale, and in view of the lack of sophisticated machinery for construction, Herculean in execution. The sluiceway and old bund at Maduru Oya rank in the forefront of these works. Several unique features of this structure testify to the sophisticated level of engineering practiced by the ancients'.

Modern Sri Lankans, who had to obtain loans from the World Bank and other aid agencies and hire foreign consulting engineers and firms for their major construction works were humbled by the achievements of their ancient ancestors. Heroic Sinhala kings with resonating Sanskrit names like Mahasen, Gajabahu, Parakramabahu, built giant irrigation works and Buddhist temples and monasteries which were wonders of the ancient world while warding off the continuing incursions of South Indian invaders. The numerous ancient irrigation schemes that dot the landscape of the Northern and Eastern plains of the country show that the giant ancestors of today's Sri Lankans had the management and organizational skills which are so lacking today.

The Minister decided that the ancient ruins should be preserved and moved the new dam site to another point.

The ghosts of the past continued to haunt us in this region and showed how much stronger they were than us. The STC managers working in these forests informed me that a place of Buddhist veneration had been discovered on a mountaintop in the jungle. I proceeded to the area with a number of the STC managers and looked up at a steep mountain covered with thick jungle. I looked around but none of the senior staff were willing to make the arduous climb. Accompanied by the younger men, I laboured up the mountain and was overcome with wonder when we arrived at a large cave which had been home to a family of bears. In the background was a perfectly proportioned statue of a sleeping Buddha about 10 meters in length, carved out of rock and still covered with a kind of white lime paint, glowing with peace and beauty in these wild surroundings.

Over the next two years, STC sales and profits continued to rise. The year before the new management took office, annual sales were Rs 40.0 million. In the first year of the new management, 1979, it was Rs 109.4 million. In the second year, 1980, it was Rs 299.5 million. In the third year, 1981, it was Rs 346.9 million. The Net Profit Before tax was minus Rs 3.9 million in 1978, the previous year. In 1979 it was a profit of Rs 29.2 million. In 1980 it was Rs 89.3 million. In 1981 it was Rs 61.4 million. This was not achieved by cutting jobs, for which the prevailing euphemism is *restructuring*. The number of employees also rose: 1,597 in 1979, 2,604 in 1980 and 2,725 in 1981.[1]

The profits brought new benefits for employees and the shareholders, the government. Again, both in 1980 and in 1981,

[1] All figures are from the STC Annual Reports.

employee salaries were increased by an average of 30 per cent. The STC in 1979 introduced a meal allowance for employees so that they could arrange their midday meal. The STC paid an allowance and left it to the employees at each workplace to decide how meals should be obtained. In offices, employees usually contracted with a catering firm. In forest working areas, employees hired cooks and set up their own kitchens. This eliminated the possibility of complaints about the quality of the food. In my experience, employees always complain about the food prepared and served in company canteens to employees.

The STC then provided all employees with two sets of clothing annually. Men received two safari suits and two pairs of shoes. The safari suits were made to measure and ordered by the head of each local workplace who hired a local tailor to make the suits to individual measurements. The cloth was purchased in bulk by the STC from a local textile company. The safari suits were light grey in colour, the same colour as the safari suits that I wore to office every day. Female employees received two saris and two pairs of sandals.

The motive for allocating two sets of clothing for all employees was never publicized: it was presented as another act of goodwill by the management. I believed that clothes made a difference to the workplace. Manual workers in Sri Lanka at the time usually wore sarongs or short trousers at work. The sarong, which normally extends to the ankles and flops about loosely, is unsuited for manual work. Workers compromise by raising the sarong above the knees which at work is unsightly and sometimes obscene. Shoes were rarely worn by manual workers. They were barefooted or wore floppy slippers. I had the notion that Western clothing would make workers more conscious of the dignity of their workplace and make them more attuned to the discipline and ways of an industrial society.

There were no females employed in manual work at the STC. In the office atmosphere, I regarded the traditional sari as the most elegant dress for a Sri Lankan woman.

The biggest benefit was awarded in 1981. The state mandated retirement benefit for all employees in Sri Lanka is the state-owned

Employees' Provident Fund. Employees pay 6 per cent of their salary and the employer contributes another 6 per cent. This retirement benefit was losing money in real terms as inflation was rising annually by about 15 per cent, while the interest earned on the deposits was low, eroding any anticipated returns. The STC decided to create a special retirement fund for all employees. Each employee would have a savings deposit account in the bank into which the equivalent of an additional 20 per cent of the salary would be paid-in by the STC, with no additional contribution by the employee. These long-term savings accounts were yielding interest rates of around 20–22 per cent per annum at the time. These monies would accumulate and would be paid back to the employees on retirement. If an employee left the STC earlier on his or her own accord, the benefit would be lost and would be divided among the others. This retirement benefit would give even the lowest grade of employees a substantial nest egg, in addition to the Provident Fund.

In 1981, shortly after STC employee salaries were increased, the government of Sri Lanka mandated that governing boards of government business corporations would not be permitted to increase employee salaries, unless sanctioned by the government. This may have had some relation to the attitude of the government trade union branch in the STC. The main office bearers from the headquarters of this trade union met the STC board of directors and expressed their concern at the grant of so many benefits to employees of the STC. They said that this embarrassed their position in other government corporations where the managements were unable to provide such benefits.

The government also received more revenue from the STC. The STC was mandated to pay 10 per cent of its revenue to the government as a royalty payment for the privilege of logging in state forests, apart from the usual corporate taxes. Because of increasing profits, the STC acceded to a request by the Department of Public Enterprises in the Ministry of Finance in 1980 and raised the STC payment of this royalty from 10 per cent to 20 per cent. Corporate tax payments increased from no payment in 1978, because of losses, to

Rs 14.6 million in 1979, Rs 43.9 million in 1980 and Rs 33.8 in 1981. By 1881, the STC had Rs 90 million in fixed long-term bank deposits and no debts to any financial institution.

The increase in revenue increased the appetite of those wanting to milk the corporation for their ends. One such person was already on the board of the STC as a nominee of the MP for Moratuwa, the furniture manufacturing centre of Sri Lanka. He was a small-time local politician who was an organizer for the Moratuwa MP. He came to meet me and made an appeal, backed by his MP and our minister, asking for a regular salary, despite his being only an honorary board member. Non-working directors customarily received only an allowance for attendance at board meetings. To avoid any complications over a minor issue, I authorized a managerial level salary for him. He then wanted an official car. This was allowed. But this only whetted his appetite for more. We then came to learn that he was visiting work points and selling special permits for luxury timber purchases. He had copied the STC timber permit for the issue of big lots of luxury timber for industrialists and his family was doing a business selling these to local people for a fee.

This caused dissatisfaction among the operations managers. I called him up and warned him against these practices. He was always very charming in my presence and had invited my family on two occasions to his house for dinner and musical evenings and introduced us to his family.[2] But he would not change his ways and presented the management with a difficult problem. The problem was solved for us by a private timber dealer operating a STC sales franchise. The Director had come with a man who had bought one of his timber permits to this dealer and demanded a large stock of luxury timber. The dealer was a tough old man who told him that his permit was invalid. An argument ensued and became heated and abusive. The director threatened the dealer and the dealer then

---

[2] The residents of the town of Moratuwa are famous in Sri Lanka for their popular music, especially the *baila*, a form of Afro-Latin music and dance inherited from the Portuguese who were in the country in the 16th and 17th centuries.

slapped him and drove him out of the premises, threatening to use his elephant in the timber yard to pulverise his car.

The managers were jubilant but were worried about my reaction to this insulting behaviour by a franchise dealer. They sent the dealer to meet me. He came to my office and humbly apologised for his behaviour. I told him he should avoid violence at all times but that I could see that he was provoked beyond limits. He was relieved and thanked me. This incident provided me with the opportunity to tell our minister that I didn't want this director on the STC board because his conduct was unbecoming of his office and this incident had made him a subject of ridicule among employees. He told me to consult the MP for Moratuwa who had sponsored the director. I told the MP that this director was a disgrace and that he only brought the MP also into disrepute. This paved the way for his removal and the appointment by the minister of a leading lawyer from the same town who was later the President of the Bar Association of Sri Lanka. This was an excellent choice.

18

GETTING PEOPLE TO WORK

WE OFTEN HEAR TOP MANAGERS IN COUNTRIES LIKE SRI LANKA complain to friends and associates: 'I can't get anything done properly in the company with these people today. Employees are so lazy and incompetent. I have to do almost everything myself.' It is not intended to be a mere description of a situation: it is an assertion of how good the top manager considers himself to be. Such egotists are among the ranks of the unrepentant incompetents. In later years as a management consultant, if a CEO made such an assertion to me, I would not consent to work for the company.

In my experience, developing countries do not necessarily have bad workers, barring the exceptional oddity. The exceptional levels of productivity of workers in the garment industry in Sri Lanka and the rest of Asia, apart from the phenomenal productivity of the Chinese and other Asians in all sorts of high technology manufacturing industries, bear witness to this. There are ineffective or incompetent managers, primarily because the tradition of business and industrial management is new to some developing countries emerging from largely agrarian economies.

Training in a proper business environment can work wonders. The STC managers proved to be exceptionally capable when given the systems and the authority to manage on their own. I could proudly say that their level of managerial skill and commitment to work and results was much higher than that of managers in the multinational corporation I had worked for earlier.

The Operations Division of the STC, in particular, had some extraordinarily able managers, led by the burly Chief Operations Manager, Henry Perera. Henry was a larger than life character in many ways. He had the loyalty and respect of his subordinates because he was both kindly and demanding. I developed a great respect for these foresters who were outdoor men at home in the Sri Lankan wilds with a deep knowledge of the local forests. Henry reviewed performances in the regions with his managers every week and only came to me if he had a problem with finances or politicians.

The oft repeated racial slur that 'the natives are lazy' has also been disproved by the astonishing economic success of Asian immigrants to the West and the recent phenomenal growth of many Asian economies.

No organization can function effectively without some basic company planning. The work plan focuses on the objectives of the company on the basis of the management's vision. Operational objectives are made specific and time-bound. Strategies that will make the objectives achievable are documented, such as capital investment, sourcing technology, training, research and product development, marketing investments, etc. And to make these realistic and workable, employees at different levels are involved in the initial processes of the plan, though the top management has to decide on the final shape of the plans based on their ambitions and available resources as perceived by them. The objectives of the plan provide the targets to be achieved by different sections within the corporation, provided the agreed inputs are made available.

The STC, like other state corporations, had no formal business plan. It had a set of financial projections made out by the Chief Accountant. This was quite common in my experience of developing countries. It also stated the capital requirements and subsidies needed from the government through the appropriations made by the line ministry from the Annual Government Budget to be approved by parliament. There were no planning or performance monitoring units in the corporation. The collection of information from the 10 regional offices and other work points were so lackadaisical that our 1978 annual report with financial performance statements were eventually completed only by mid 1979, and that too only after additional accountants were recruited to help with the work. It is not uncommon for state enterprises to publish their annual reports six months from the legally due date of 31 March of the following year; and in extreme cases after more than a year. How very different from the workings of the multinational corporation where the top managers would get the cumulative sales and gross profit figures for individual products weekly.

A planning officer was recruited. Though this young lady had no experience of corporate planning, such people being virtually unavailable in the country for recruitment to the public sector, she had a university degree in statistics and a ready willingness to learn. Additional Accounts Managers were also recruited. The board of directors then worked out the corporate goals and set out the broad objectives for the next five years. The 10 regional managers were then asked to work out their production and sales capacities by products, based on the new opportunities for harvesting timber in the Mahaweli Area and in the cyclone damaged teak plantations in the Eastern Province.

After several meetings with the regional managers, the plan was finalised and approved by the board, and given to all senior managers. The plan was a fairly bulky document, as the STC handled a large variety of species of timber and different timber products such as sawn timber, firewood, transmission poles, railroad sleepers. Each product had a separate set of figures indicating proposed sales figures, financial returns and investments. It also proposed to invest in several new products such as household doors, windows, wall panels and floor panels.

Based on these figures, each regional manager agreed on monthly production and sales targets. Monitoring these performances was the key to improved performance. Meetings were held on the 10th day of each month to review the performance of the previous month, when all performance statistics had been collected and printed into a monthly performance report. To highlight the importance of these meetings that lasted two full days, they were held at the Taprobane Hotel in Colombo, with participants enjoying all meals during the period at the hotel. The first day was devoted to an explanation of the variances between targets and performances by each manager. If there were shortfalls, the manager had to come up with the proposed solution. These were discussed and, since they usually had financial implications, were approved by me and my approval was recorded.

For example, a manager would say that he had large stocks of an item but the demand at the time in the region was lower than expected. There were often other regional managers who were willing to receive these stocks as their local demand was higher. Sometimes, the quality of the timber harvested would be below expected standards and the manager would ask for a special discounted sale price. Or managers would say that there was a need to advertise certain products to stimulate sales or offer a promotional price for a period of time.

What was astonishing was the change in the personality of the managers. At the first few meetings, when individual managers were called upon to put up their regional performances against targets on a large screen from a projector, they were too timid to speak up or make any suggestions in the presence of the Chairman and Working Director. In the tradition of the country, people were intimidated by the presence of the head of the organisation. I had to patiently encourage them. I repeatedly stated that I had no knowledge of the business in each region or of forestry in general and if I did make a proposal that did not make sense, I expected the managers to tell me that I was wrong. Anyone who agreed with me just to please me was not doing me any favours. Frank discussion would be the basis of these operational decisions. After a few months, the atmosphere was cordial and discussions were frank.

The second day was devoted to training. I would take a session on a management subject in the morning or we would have an external specialist to present a topic. The evening was devoted to a presentation on some aspect of forestry or a forestry related subject which an individual manager had to present to the house. Each manager was allocated a turn to make a presentation and was free to choose his own subject after discussion with the Chief Operations Manager. The financial resources to carry out the required research and equipment such as video cameras and other equipment were made available. The quality of the presentations was uniformly of a very high standard. It is my lasting regret that I did not have these presentations published in book form.

After a few months, there was a very visible change in the personalities of the managers. People were becoming confident and accepting responsibility for results. Managers would be ashamed to come before all their colleagues and confess that they had failed in some area of work and tried their best or came prepared with suggestions to overcome a difficult situation. On the second day, after work was over, drinks and dinner were on the house. The Working Director and I would sit with the managers and the other participants and have beer and exchange stories. This created an exceptional team spirit that bonded the group on a personal level.

The Planning Office received the performance data from each regional operational office at the end of each working day. These figures were collated and the sales performance of the organization was available on my desk every morning. Since phone services in some of the more remote regions of the country were poor, the STC hired Motorola to install a radio communication system between the main STC operational offices and the Planning Office for daily transmission of information.

It was not uncommon in the public sector, where management standards had declined over the years, for lower level employees to seek private interviews with the head of the organization to ask for redress of grievances, by-passing their immediate supervisors. It was also quite common to receive anonymous letters accusing people of wrong doing, based on personal grudges. I sent out circulars to all employees stating that the chain of command had to be respected before matters were brought to me. An employee had to first complain to his or her supervisor. If this was not satisfactory, it should be taken up with the manager of the department. If this was still not resolved, the employee could come to me with his manager and supervisor, by prior appointment. Anonymous letters were also banned: all such letters would be destroyed without being read.

I found that the most effective way of encouraging employees was to visit them at their work points and hold meaningful discussions and establish a line of communication. I spent a good deal of time each month visiting the different work points in the country. I would arrive at some remote work station and first have tea and talk to the manager or supervisor in charge of the place. Then we would go around the work point and see the men at work, asking questions and getting answers all the time. At the end of this walk around, it would be close to lunch time. Since employee meals were financed by the STC and each work point had a dining area, I would join the workers at lunch and exchange pleasantries with those around me.

After lunch, I would call a meeting and address the workers. I would dwell on the latest financial performance of the STC, noting that our business performance was among the best in the country. I would then invite questions and suggestions for performance improvement. At initial meetings, workers would grouse about poor facilities: leaky roofs or taps, absence of drinking water at work stations, etc. I would then turn to the officer-in-charge and tell him that he had full authority to provide these facilities without reference to higher management and that this was his province. At subsequent meetings, the tone was usually different. After my talk, a workers' representative would get up and thank me and say: 'Sir, you have more ability than any of us. You lead the way and we will follow.'

One encounter with the employees was quite different. One of the largest STC work places was at Boosa, a few miles before arriving in Galle on the coast road to the south. There were about 200 employees here working in the treatment plants for transmission poles and railroad sleepers, apart from sawmilling and kiln drying. I had failed to visit this location during my first one and a half years. I informed the General Manager one morning that I wanted him to accompany me to Boosa on a work visit. The General Manager's response was a bit discouraging.

'I am sorry, Sir. No senior manager from the head office will visit Boosa. The workers there are very rough and dangerous characters. You know, these coastline people of the South are notoriously violent but these chaps are special. They carry swords and knives and are ever ready to use these in any altercation. I cannot go to that place.' I decided to forego this visit and forgot the incident in the rush of other work.

Some months later, a representative delegation of workers from Boosa wanted to see me. I met them in my office and was convinced that they must have some grievance to air. They came in quietly and sat down and the spokesman said: 'Sir, we heard the news that you wanted to pay us a visit and that the General Manager discouraged you from making that visit. Our workers were very sorry to hear this. We are here as their representatives to invite you and your wife to pay us a visit and do us the honour of having lunch with us. Please give us a date that is convenient for you.'

A visit was arranged and I went there with my wife. As a lookout from the workplace saw our car approaching this large complex, the main gate was opened and we entered the large compound. The entire roadway from the gate to the office building was lined on either side by workers in two orderly rows, dressed in their grey safari suits, standing to attention as though they were at an army parade. When we arrived at the office, which was decorated with flags, the supervisory staff and the union leaders greeted us in traditional style with the offering of a sheaf of betel leaves. We had drinks of sodas and coconut water and then went around the workplace to inspect the machines and the work that was being done. They were proud to show us what they were doing and made suggestions for expanding facilities.

Afterwards, we all had a heavy lunch of biryani rice and chicken curry. Microphones had been set up and a stage erected for a meeting and the lunch was followed by many laudatory speeches and expressions of goodwill. I responded to these in kind. The atmosphere was that of a village wedding celebration. Naturally, both my wife and I were moved by such a genuine show of appreciation.

Sri Lanka has a long tradition of working class agitation, initiated in the early 1930s by communist and other left-wing political parties. The condition of workers, at the time, was very much in need of improvement. As the rural population of the country kept expanding, landless peasants were forced to seek work in plumbago mines, industries and tea and rubber plantations under harsh conditions. These workers were unionized by left-wing parties that carried out a constant agitation through strikes, demonstrations and other forms of trade union action for better working conditions while employers, backed by the government, used the police and other government instruments to block these agitations. Worker agitations led to legislation that eventually provided for better working conditions in Sri Lanka than in the rest of South Asia.

Despite these appearances of class war, these South Asian societies still have another vestige of traditional agrarian societies: intense loyalty to leaders whom they have put their faith in. Unlike workers in industrialized Western societies, whose relationship with the top management is generally impersonal, workers in these societies respond very positively to an interactive relationship. But it is quite different from the concept of popularity in Western societies. The outward familiarity that is evident in an American workplace, where workers will address the boss by the first name, is not the correct form in this traditional society. Superiors are addressed formally by employees with respectful titles: without such respect discipline will break down. Even a superior speaking to a subordinate must use a formal manner, addressing the person either by the job title or some other impersonal form.[1]

---

[1] Robert Knox, the most perceptive of foreign writers on Sri Lanka in the 17th century, notes: 'It is an affront and shame to them to be called by those (personal) names, which they say is to be like unto dogs.'

Apart from salary and other benefits, concern extends to better human relationships. During my tenure in the STC, two employees died under tragic circumstances, unrelated to their work in the STC. On both occasions, I went with a team of senior managers to their humble dwellings, even though they were located in remote areas where we had to leave our vehicles and walk some distance. On both occasions, I had instructed the Chief Accountant to come with me with a tidy sum in cash which he gave the bereaved wives as ex-gratia payments from the STC so that these would cover the funeral arrangements and leave something to spare till the other benefits became available.

I had a glimpse of this style of management in my own youth. My own father was the Works Manager at the large government factory in Kolonnawa when he died just prior to retirement. He was a very popular manager in the workplace. Almost every working day at the factory, he started work by walking through the entire extensive factory area, talking to the workers and checking on the progress of the work. I would accompany him occasionally when I had my school holidays. He knew most workers by their names. It is only then that he returned to the office to do the day's paper work and meetings. When he died prematurely, the representatives of the four thousand workers in the factory informed our family that the funeral arrangements would be made by the workers. They declared the day a holiday, made the funeral arrangements and carried the coffin on their shoulders for six miles to the cemetery where they had erected the funeral pyre.

Managements have a great opportunity to tap into this reservoir of goodwill that the less sophisticated and less complicated societies of developing countries can provide. This goodwill can be a force for increased productivity and a peaceful work environment.

19

RE-PROGRAMMING PEOPLE

IN MY SECOND YEAR, IN 1980, I HAD TIME TO VISIT SALES DEPOTS AND spend time observing salesmanship of the public sector variety. I would arrive at a STC sales depot and observe the people at work to familiarise myself with the procedures and the organization. I would walk around the timber yards with the depot supervisor and ask him about the different species of timber, the availability of each and the sales potential. There were many times when a supervisor would reply that he was uncertain of a species of timber that was being unloaded into the yard by a logging contractor. I would then ask him, 'If you don't know the species, how do pay him?' The contractor is paid on the basis of the species of timber and its girth and length. The reply was always, 'We ask the contractor for the information if we don't know the species. They know these things very well.'

The STC had about 225 people categorized as supervisors, overseeing work in the forest felling areas. This large number was required because most of the logging was done by private logging contractors whose work had to be supervised at different points. It was not sensible for the STC to have a large permanent workforce for this project as logging areas were not predictable, as it was dependent on the Forest Department which never had a comprehensive work plan for harvesting the forests.

People working in the sales and supervisory grades could not be effective if they were not knowledgeable about timber species and their characteristics. In the early days, when the STC was formed in 1968 out of the Sales Division of the Forest Department, the employees received some training at the Department's School of Forestry. Over time, as the STC expanded, new recruits were brought in and were expected to learn on the job, as is usual in Sri Lanka. Such learning is limited in scope and the need to get the job done resulted in the case mentioned.

When this issue was discussed at the next management meeting, the first thought was to send supervisors for training at the Forest Department's training school in Trincomalee. But the numbers were too large for the school, which in any case was already under-funded and having its own problems. The managers then proposed the idea of the STC setting up a school of forestry studies. We were told that there were many competent management grade retirees from the Forest Department whose talents were now being wasted and could be recruited as teachers. The Forest Department's oper-ational managers were at the time qualified foresters, mostly trained in the Indian School of Forestry in Madras, while others had post-graduate training in the UK.

Once the proposal for a school was approved, I moved out to concentrate on other tasks. T.B. Wettewe, who had been up-graded from Working Director to Vice-Chairman, and the Chief Oper-ations Manager, Henry Perera, were in charge of the project. About three months later, I was told that the school was functioning. I travelled to the location in the heart of the Mahaweli area, a village called Pimburathewa, an STC base camp in the Maduru Oya area, about 150 miles from Colombo in the Eastern Province forests, and was amazed by what had been achieved. Temporary buildings dotted a cleared area.

The school was equipped with classrooms, teaching equipment, a small library, living quarters and a bus. There were 30 supervisors at study. They were undergoing a three week intensive course. As in an army training school, students were up at 4.00 a.m. on some days and travelling by bus to different forest areas to identify trees. They returned by noon, when it was becoming too hot for outdoor study, and began classroom work. Studies continued till very late in the evening. There was no time for relaxation. At the end of three weeks, they had a written examination and a practical test. When they passed, there was a graduation ceremony and I would personally attend the ceremonial award of certificates.

Students who failed were informed that they could participate in the course again and try to qualify. Those who did not qualify were told that they would not be considered for salary increases or promotions. I liked the idea of army-style intensive training where students had to work so hard that they silently cursed the trainers but learnt a lot in a short time and were proud of their achievements when the course ended.

Formal two week training courses were also held for Coupe Officers (as supervisors at felling points were called), for Assistant Regional Managers and Deputy Regional Managers. Senior managers had courses at the National Institute of Business Management in Colombo while others went on foreign training courses. Usually, only higher level officers were sent abroad for training. During this period the STC sent foremen working in sawmills to Malaysia for training in sawmilling, despite the reservations of the ministry officials who felt that workers who did not speak English could not be trained abroad. Work standards visibly improved over time.

What was truly astonishing was the innovative spirit of the operations managers and their ability to get these done so efficiently when they were given the resources and the freedom to work. In my 15 years in the multinational corporation, I did not come across managers who were so highly motivated and effective as these public service managers. Sadly, I learnt a few years later that, after I had left the STC, the next CEO had shut down the training school stating that it was an unnecessary extravagance on the part of his predecessor.

Another visit to a sales depot of the STC set us off on a new project of a different sort. Arriving early morning at a sales depot close to Colombo, I sat down to watch what was being done by the employees.

About 10 trucks had arrived and were parked outside the gates of the premises. The depot officer was busy making entries in journals and log books. He then went out and informed the customers in the last five trucks in the queue to go away and come back the next day.

This astonished me and I asked him why he was turning away customers who had come with hundreds of thousands of rupees in cash to buy goods. The stocks were there. Customers paid in cash as the STC did not accept cheques at sales points. The point was, the depot officer said, that there were so many documents and registers to enter that he had no time to deal with more than five customers daily. I counted the registers on his table: there were 21 in all.

I called a meeting of the senior managers and raised this issue. The information that the registers contained may have been important but these could not be as important as selling the goods and making sales revenue. I demanded that the procedure be cut to down to 20 per cent of the existing level. The Chief Internal Auditor was given the task of studying the procedure and recommending a new one.

Internal and external auditors in the public sector walk a tightrope. The public sector is replete with the abuse of authority by powerful persons but it is usually too risky to highlight these. So the auditors make up for it by being very severe on the small people. In the STC, the Internal Auditors would make monthly visits to timber yards and sales points and report that Rs 50 worth of timber could not be accounted for in the books, in locations where stocks worth millions of rupees were held. The former management would then impose fines on the supervisors in charge. I stopped these punishments since they forced supervisors to be more concerned with book entries than sales. Timber perishes at times or these may be wrongly classified regarding size or quality. There are a host of reasons why large timber stocks cannot be exactly counted and valued and there had to be a plus or minus allowance of at least a few thousand rupees when checking stocks.

The Chief Internal Auditor's report was even more disturbing. Auditors are usually at odds with operational people in many organizations. But to investigate and conclude that the controls were still insufficient for proper accountability was hard to accept without becoming disillusioned with the auditing profession. The only solution was to seek external help from a region where people knew that the priority of a business was to secure more customers and make more sales and profits. The American Executive Service Corps provided just the right man.

This was a remarkable gentleman who taught many of us some good lessons in management and personal relations. Before his retirement from work in the USA, he had been the Vice-President/Finance in a large US corporation. In preparation for his arrival, the STC had constructed a special office for him in the Accounts Department building, with air-conditioning and expensive office furniture. It was also the practice for the beneficiary of Executive Service Corps services to provide the expert and his wife with accommodation in a luxury hotel during his stay. This gentleman visited me in my home on arrival and informed me that he would be more comfortable in a small house in the city where his wife could do the house-keeping, a type of accommodation that would be much less expensive. He also told me that he would not use the luxury room, as he did not want to make a special distinction with the other STC managers and would be content to occupy a desk like any of them.

His style was very different from our previous experiences with American managers. After visiting work sites and making studies of the numerous accounting books, he was able to simplify the procedures by eliminating the numerous duplication of information. He came to my office one day and showed me an STC invoice form. He asked me, 'Do you know how old this type of form is?' I had to say that I had never thought of it, or for that matter even seen the form before.

'This invoice was designed by the British government about sixty years ago,' he said. 'It is still used in public departments. Since some of the requirements have changed, rubber stamps are made on the form to modify the document but the old format is the one that is still printed and available.'

I expressed shock but I knew that this was how the public sector worked. Old forms were discarded and a few new ones substituted. For example, when payments were made, there were entries recorded in several ledgers. He eliminated many of these by having an extension area on each cheque leaf of the STC cheque books where the payment approvals could be recorded so that there was no need for transferring payment information to other books. He also told me that the banks should have the name of the STC on the cheque leaf. Since all these changes were new to the Sri Lankan banks, he went personally to meet the heads of the banks to make the changes. It is much easier for a foreigner to influence top officials in Sri Lanka than for a Sri Lankan.

The most remarkable feature of his style was his modesty, designed to make sure his work was implemented. He visited me at home in the early days of his work when he had designed some of his improvements. He told me that I should summon meetings to discuss these changes and that at these meetings I should not refer to him even though he was present. I should start by informing the meeting that our Chief Accountant and Chief Internal Auditor, and their staffs, had come up with new ideas for improving documentation. I should give my staff all the credit and congratulate them. In this way, they would be pleased to implement the changes. Amazingly, this strategy worked very well.

His work earned for the STC uncounted millions of rupees in sales and profits in the years to come. When the Director of Public Enterprises in the Ministry of Finance heard about these changes, he was very interested. Mr Somasunderam was an exceptional public officer and one of the most brilliant public servants I have met. He made the effort to improve public enterprise management both in Sri Lanka and later as an international expert in other countries. He wanted me to provide lectures to other public enterprises on the new accounting systems at the STC. Since our American expert had left the country by then, I had to admit that I was not competent for that task as I had no professional training as an accountant.

A third improvement that became necessary was to develop a new corporate culture where promotions would be based on merit and not on seniority, favour or political influence. It was decided that promotion to supervisory grades and from supervisory grades to management should be based, at least in part, on knowledge of the work requirements. Hence, candidates for promotion were required to sit for a written examination and only those who qualified were interviewed for selection. The Vice-Chairman, T.B. Wettewe, took charge of this project with the assistance of the Personnel Manager. To make these selections processes more interesting, I noted that many of these tests were held in the provincial towns where the STC had offices while the candidates were put up in local Rest Houses.[1]

---

[1] Rest Houses are government-owned lodging houses. These were first established in the colonial times for the benefit of public servants traveling to the provinces on duty.

20

MORE ENCOUNTERS WITH POLITICIANS

WHEN HARVARD BUSINESS SCHOOL PREPARED A CASE STUDY ON MY part in the dramatic transformation of the STC (Ref. N9-390-104 of 4/17/90, Harvard Business School case studies), it focussed strongly on my work in establishing a successful communication with the external organizations the STC would have to interact with to develop new systems and seek new business opportunities. A major issue was the interface with powerful politicians. However, the full story was too sensitive to be revealed at the time the case study was being prepared by the representative of the business school who came on a fact finding mission to Sri Lanka. But it is a story that has to be told now. Many of the actors are no longer in positions of power, and some, including the former minister, are now deceased. He was killed by a terrorist bomb during a public meeting in a subsequent year.

The extent of the political dimension in business in Sri Lanka, as in many other developing countries, is important to understand. Sri Lanka inherited an independent public service from the British during colonial times. Many senior public servants were British at one time and an independent Public Service Commission governed appointments, promotions and transfers. During the early years of independence, this tradition continued. Senior civil servants of that era, disillusioned by later developments, would nostalgically relate how they declined improper requests by the Prime Minister and senior cabinet ministers on grounds that these were contrary to public service regulations. All this changed after the populist 'Peoples' Government' came into power in 1956.

Sri Lanka (Ceylon at the time) was given universal adult franchise for elections to the legislature, the State Council, by the British Labour-Liberal government of the time as far back as 1931, while still a Crown Colony, making it the first to achieve this democratic right in Asia. Leading local politicians, who all came from the affluent upper classes, had opposed this proposal, except for a few left-wing radicals. This exposure to democracy led to numerous social benefits which were far ahead of those in other developing countries. Even before independence in 1948, Sri Lanka had universal free education including university education, free public health services, legislative safeguards for workers, etc.

Democratic political institutions designed on the British model function on the basis of gentlemanly codes of conduct based on middle-class social values of British origin. Political opponents treat each other with respect. They argue, with studied politeness, and differ on issues, but do not work to destroy their opponents or use political power to gain undue advantages. These codes of behaviour were understood by the Anglicized Sri Lankan middle class that dominated politics in the early years. But it did not permeate into the rural society where the vast majority of Sri Lankans lived under different traditional values.

The local administration of rural Sri Lanka, even in British times, was based on traditional village leaders whose positions were legitimised by the government. There were village headmen, *korale mahattayas, vidanay arachchies,* and such others who held power in the villages and carried on the traditions inherited from medieval Sri Lanka under its old kingdoms, so long as they did not openly conflict with the laws of the national government. The Peoples' Government of 1956 brought in many people from this stratum of society in rural Sri Lanka into parliament. Once in power, they tended to behave as they did in rural Sri Lanka, with a lack of respect for the traditions of British parliamentary democracy.

The extension of political power from the Anglicized urban middle class to the rural people may be one step forward, but it also took the country two steps back. The value system changed. Politicians behaved like medieval lords and imposed their will on the public service. Existing public service regulations were ignored or systematically changed. Many senior public officers retired or were forced into retirement and a new breed of public servants servile to politicians replaced them.

One Member of Parliament for Kandy and a senior cabinet minister famously said, and was reported in the media, that 'If you have the government you must rule like the king.'[1]

Powers acquired by any group of people are rarely surrendered. With each successive government, politicians strengthened their powers over the public administration for their own benefit. Political opponents were intimidated. The tone of debates in parliament itself changed.

This was the climate we worked in. Going through the operational plans of the STC with the Chief Operations Manager in our first few months, the Working Director and I came upon an unusual stumbling block to operations in one region. The Forest Department was in charge of state forests and, even though the Conservator of Forests, as its head was known, was a member of the Board of Directors of the STC, the department was very conscious of its role as the guardian of the forests and was very sparing in allocating forest felling areas. One rich forest region, allocated only for selective felling of marked mature trees, was an area in the central regions called Laggala. After the new government was elected, the Member of Parliament (MP) for the area had claimed the privilege of personally appointing contractors to log the forest for the STC. This contravened all established government procedures. Established procedure laid down that logging contractors had to obtain 'worth certificates' from the provincial Government Agent[2] testifying to

---

[1] In the Sinhala language, the word for *government* approximates with the word for *king*.

[2] The government agent in Sri Lanka is the head of the provincial administration of the government.

their business assets as the work needed assets in the form of trucks for transport, experienced loggers, offices, elephants for drawing logs from the forest and trucks for the transport of logs to the STC yards. These approved contractors then made bids for the work and were selected by the Operations management. If this work was delegated to an MP, a situation that was contrary to all established business practice, it was quite likely that the timber harvest would end up privately in the market and not in the STC yards.

To the credit of the former Chairman and the General Manager, the STC had refused to bow to the MPs incessant demands. Unable to resist the political pressure, they had chosen to leave out the Laggala forests from their work plans. I took a confrontational line and ordered that tenders should be called for work in the area from approved contractors in accordance with established procedures.

The reaction came within a few days. The MP arrived at my office with about a dozen of his minions, who would be the beneficiaries of his largesse, and had a meeting with me. He was a small man but had the reputation of being a rough character. I called in the Working Director and the Chief Operations Manager but did all the talking for the STC as their positions would be vulnerable to political pressures even at a future date. I told him that the established procedures would be followed. The MP insisted that his people could handle the logging and that he, as the elected Member of Parliament for his constituency, had the right to choose the people who worked on government contracts in his area. This was in accord with a growing movement in national politics that allowed MPs to behave like feudal chiefs in the historical times of the Sinhala kings. I contended that this was the role of the STC management, not the local MP. All this was conducted with studied civility: I addressed the MP with the honorific *Manthri Thuma* while he addressed me as *Sabhapathi Thuma*.[3] Since the MP could make no headway, he told me that he would take the matter to my superior, the Minister of Lands and Land Development, and left.

---

[3] *Sabhapathi Thuma* translates into Honourable Chairman and *Manthri Thuma* into Honourable Member of Parliament.

A few days later he was back with his team. He was more sub-
dued and complained: 'Even the Honourable Minister says that
he is not willing to countermand you. But you must remember Sir,
that you are seated in that chair as the chairman of this business only
because we fought and won the parliamentary elections to establish
this government, extending to confrontations with the opposition
that involved fighting and murder.'

'Manthri Thuma is making a big mistake,' I said, 'I have a good
career as the head of a department in the very large XYZ multinational company where my salary was five times that of a chairman
of a government corporation. I have made a big sacrifice to temporarily join the public sector at the earnest pleading of the Honourable Minister. If I feel that the government is not interested in my
work, I will leave this place any moment and revert to my former
employment.'

He became contrite: 'Pardon me, Sir. My tongue made a mistake.'[4]
That ended the direct opposition to the work and logging contracts
were assigned as usual for work in that forest region. Some petty
local harassment of the STC employees still continued in the area
but the principle had been established and a message was being
sent out by the STC.

Some other encounters were not as simple to resolve. The MP
for Panduvasnuwara, an ancient Sinhala city of historical signifi-
cance, came with the request for a donation of a large quantity of
teak timber for the reconstruction of some ancient temples. Why
such requests should come from the MP of the area and why he
should be the purchaser of material and not the construction engineers will only be understood in the context of the politics in
Sri Lanka. Such requests are difficult to refuse as they wear the
guise of public interest. This was followed by similar requests from
the MP for Kandy for the restoration of religious sites in his
constituency. Even though the senior managers informed me

---

[4] It is a traditional Sinhala phrase where a speaker tries to withdraw an accu-
sation by faulting his tongue, thereby exonerating himself, as though he and his
tongue were two different persons.

privately that the MP was constructing a large house for himself at the same time, the request could not be turned down. Such requests were acceded to as there was no need to create political animosity when there were more important tasks at hand for us.

Some requests were so blatantly fraudulent that they had to be refused. The government at the time was engaged in several large public-works which made some business people who had befriended ministers into multi-millionaires. One such enterprising gentleman owned a large timber mill just north of Colombo. He was involved in building thousands of rural houses for a massive low-income housing project spearheaded by the Prime Minister who had made this one of his key development projects. But the gentleman was also a good friend of our chief, the Minister of Lands and Land Development, who was strong political rival of the Prime Minister. He had also given him contracts to build houses for expatriate engineers working in the new Mahaweli hydro-electric power projects.

This gentleman came to see me one day. He was elegantly attired as usual in an impeccably white and silky national dress of loose white shirt buttoned at the collar and white lungi. He bowed very decorously when he met me, sat down confidently and addressed me in a measured voice. '*Sabhapathi Thuma*, we are engaged in a very meritorious project for the welfare of the poor people in our country. You know that the Honourable Prime Minister has made low-income housing his lead project. We need your assistance in this matter. We need a permit to purchase 5,000 cubic feet of good teak timber at a concessionary price. I have a letter for you from the Prime Minister supporting this request.'

Locally harvested teak was in limited supply and was given on allocation to house builders and carpentry industries. The price of local teak sold by the STC was still too low to allow timber merchants to import teak from South East Asia, where it was still plentiful. Hence the demand for STC teak was very high in the local market. I responded with a smile: 'I have to tell you Sir, that no sensible person would use valuable teak wood for the construction of tiny low-income houses for poor peasants. It is not for nothing that my hair is grey!'[5]

'You are then refusing the Prime Minister's request? May I take this up with your Minister?' 'Please do that, Sir.' I responded. After a few days he came back to try his luck. 'The Honourable Minister says that he cannot interfere with your work. So are you still refusing us?' 'I am sorry to say that that is the position.' I said.

I had occasion to meet this gentleman socially on some occasions afterwards. He always remained courteous and friendly, despite our encounter over teak. Many years later, long after I had left the STC, I was very ill and was warded in the large modern hospital this gentleman had built in Colombo as part of his ever expanding business through his political contacts. He was doing the rounds of the hospital one day to check on conditions when he came to my room and saw me in bed. He greeted me warmly and expressed his concern for my health. He then called the nursing staff to that ward and gave a short speech. 'This gentleman is a very honourable man who has done a lot for this country. I want you to remember to take very special care of him.' There was a lot of decency in this complex personality.

Another encounter was with the Deputy Minister in the Ministry of Lands. A man of rustic background, he represented a farming area in the North Central Province. Gruff, swarthy and heavily built, he had a rough appearance and manner of speaking but was really a gentle man at heart. He phoned me in office and asked for what he said was a big favour. A high official in the government trade union, the JSS, was employed as a sawmill worker at the STC saw-milling yard in a Southern town called Thimbulketiya. He wanted this man promoted to the level of supervisor. I bluntly refused. I told him that we had established systems and procedures for promotion and I would not consent to by-pass these as it would create a lack of confidence in the new systems the management was implementing.

[5] A Sinhala expression meaning that a person has the wisdom of mature years when he has grey hair. I have had grey hair since the time I turned thirty.

In case of any future repercussions, I informed the Minister that I had refused this request by his Deputy.

This revelation led to an unforeseen problem. At the subsequent monthly meeting the minister had with his heads of departments, he publicly told the Deputy Minister that he should not interfere with the work of the Chairman of the STC as he was brought in to establish new management systems. I was embarrassed and I felt that this public rebuke would antagonise an important man. However, it turned out quite differently. He went on to become a personal friend and would often invite me and the family to have dinner at his residence with his family.

Despite continuing support from the minister to ward off politicians who were seeking benefits from the STC, the minister himself would try to test my resolve. He was often surrounded by a number of disreputable hangers on. These were rakes from good families who had fallen on bad times due to drink and riotous ways. The minister seemed to have a strange empathy with these fellows. He would sometimes send one of these fellows with a small scribbled note asking me to help them. They would ask for a permit for a large quantity of luxury timber, which we all understood they would sell to some timber merchant for a high price. I invariably declined the request.

There were numerous other instances at the local level when small time politicians tried to intervene in STC management affairs. In most of these cases, the energetic Working Director, who was constantly touring work places, much more than I could or wanted to do, would ward off these intrusions with a mixture of bluff and courtesy. But one cannot win all battles and still survive. When the STC was increasing its turnover and profits in my third year, the Working Director and I got a call from the minister for a private meeting. Here he stated firmly that he wanted paid employment for 20 of his dissolute cronies in the STC at executive level. He claimed that they could be designated as Public Relations Officers. They must also be provided with private cars by the STC. He could not be contradicted on this issue.

We returned with serious misgivings and summoned a meeting of the board of directors. We informed the board that we had received an illegitimate request from the minister and that we had two choices. We could accede to the minister's illegitimate order and be complicit to a serious irregularity. Or we should all resign as a board and deny the minister his request. There were many expressions of concern about the Minister's request, now virtually a demand, but the members had no intention of resigning. So we discussed how we could comply and yet save the STC management from ridicule and pacify the employees who now lay great store by our integrity. We would appoint these 20 persons as STC executives on a temporary basis and provide them with salaries and an official car, with the proviso that they should never set foot inside the STC offices or interfere with its work. This was approved by the minister. These chaps only wanted some easy income to finance their dissolute living.

There was one small hitch before the scheme was completed. The STC had bought new imported Mitsubishi cars for all its senior managers. The minister had remarked that it would have been cheaper and more expedient to buy some Fiat cars that were being assembled by a local businessman who had appealed to the minister for help in selling his rather crude vehicle (it went off the market a year later and the assembly plant was shut down). Taking advantage of this, the STC managers, who disliked this whole scheme, ordered 20 Fiat cars for these illegal entrants. On hearing this, they protested to the minister who ordered that they should also receive Mitsubishi cars.

I never met any of these playboy friends of the minister. They kept their word and kept away from the STC, only drawing salaries that were credited regularly to their bank accounts. I believe they enjoyed the STC largesse for many years, even after I had left the STC, till the Minister himself was removed from his position some years later in a cabinet reshuffle by his arch rival, the former Prime Minister and subsequent President of the country. A few years later, during the time of my successor as Chairman of the STC, some of these gentlemen were involved in a widely publicized sex scandal involving the use of STC money and facilities that eventually led to the removal of that chairman from office. The exposure of the scandal and the wide publicity it received was the result of the work of the STC trade unions that were disgusted with the abuses at the time.

It was completely normal for supervisory institutions, such as the line ministry led by the Secretary to the Ministry and the Auditor-General's Department, to refuse to see such gross violations of public service regulations and norms of conduct. In this case, 20 unnecessary posts had been created (why does a corporation need 20 PR men who have no qualifications?) and absent people were being paid salaries for doing nothing. When the Auditor-General's officers completed their government audit of the STC that year, they came to draw my attention to the shortage of some timber, worth a few thousand rupees, from some sales depots. In a mischievous mood, I told them that we had committed a far more egregious error at board level in appointing 20 PROs who received salaries and official cars without even visiting the STC, all at the bequest of the minister. Would they care to inquire into this? No, they did not want even to hear about it.

In my third year in office, I got a call from the office of the President of Sri Lanka asking me to attend a meeting in the President's office. It was the Secretary to the President, a very senior civil servant. His voice was peremptory. 'When do you want us?' I asked and was rewarded with the curt answer, 'Come here, immediately.' I sensed something untoward and assembled the General Manager, the Chief Operations Manager and the Working Director and set off for the President's office.

We arrived at the President's office and were led immediately to a conference room. The President sat at the head of the table, looking very severe, the Secretary to the President on one side and the CEO of the Parquet Company, Mr S.W., was on his other side. I realized that this businessman had been the instigator of the meeting, as he was a good friend of the President and a long-time beneficiary of his largesse, but we had no idea what game he was now playing. As we entered the room and took our seats, the President began to berate me in a loud voice: 'What do you think you are up to? You have been appointed Chairman of the Timber Corporation to fell timber and sell it, not to start all kinds of industries. What is the meaning of this business of opening a new factory? Who authorized you to do such a thing?'

The matter now became clear. The corporation was clear felling the Mahaweli Development Area and was harvesting vast quantities of varied kinds of timber. However, the Sri Lankan consumer had a very traditional view of what timber species should be used at the time. The demand was for popularly known luxury timbers like teak, mahogany, jak, and satinwood. But large quantities of excellent timber were being harvested from Mahaweli and the state forest plantations that had no market. The STC had taken out large advertisements in the local papers for these species of timber and even put out a calendar featuring some of these and their uses. But stocks of these timbers were accumulating in the yards. The STC then decided to establish a small factory to use these timbers to make wall panelling, flooring, and later, standard doors and windows for house-builders. It was hoped that the success of such a venture would encourage other manufacturers. The timbers used initially were cypress, *panakka* and *kirihembiliya*, all being timber found to be in excess of industrial demand. To establish the factory, the STC got down a specialist in manufacturing timber products from the American Executive Service Corps of the USA who did an excellent job designing the entire project.

When the news of the new factory got around, I received a call from this CEO of Parquet Company. He wanted me to abort the whole project. 'If you start this, we are going to have a lot more competition in our business. I am requesting you to halt this project.' I told him that this would not affect his business and that we needed to go ahead to get rid of some of our large stocks of what we termed 'unwanted species'. There the matter ended, or so we thought.

I was taken aback by the arrogant and unfriendly tone of the President. I humbly replied, 'Let me explain this, Sir.' He snapped back, 'I don't want your explanations. Give a yes or no answer to my question.' I spoke out firmly and said, 'I am sorry, Your Excellency. If you want an answer, you will have to listen to me.'

Since he remained silent, I continued: 'We are clear-felling the Mahaweli Development Area and some of the forest plantations. People in the country have traditionally very set ideas of what timbers to buy. While we have a scarcity of the well known luxury timber species, the large quantity of other species that are now being harvested remain unsold and are categorized as unwanted timber. Most of these are very good hardwoods but the public is unaware of their value. Industrialists are not interested in these. We have advertized these timbers for six months with poor results. The wastage of this timber is a big loss to the country. So we decided to process and sell these ourselves to make a saving for the country. Mr S.W. who is seated here knows all this as I have spoken to him on this matter. He uses only teak thinnings for his business and even when we increased timber prices two years ago we did not increase the price of teak thinnings purely to help him. He pays only Rs 15 per cubic foot for teak thinnings, a special low price exclusively for him.'

The President was quick to realize that he had been misled. So he made a joke of the whole issue by turning to the Secretary and telling him aloud, 'I say, why should S.W. get special prices from the Timber Corporation? That is not fair by the others! Don't you agree? Alright, Mr Chairman, you can go.'

As we walked out, our Minister of Lands & Land Development, who had joined the meeting without our observing it, came out and spoke to me with some concern. 'Kenneth, you are a hell of a chap. You can't talk to the President of Sri Lanka like that.' I told him, 'Sir, you know that my intentions are honest. After all that I have done with little benefit to me, I don't want to be ill treated as well.' He seemed to tolerate this obstinacy and went his way with a smile.

The new factory was established in the Ratmalana STC complex. It was very professionally laid out and had just the right machinery newly installed, all based on the drawings and plans made out by the US expert. It was a success. It continued to expand in later years, even after I had left.

The run of the mill Sri Lankan politicians are a colourful bunch of people. They are generally very eloquent and long-winded, as most Sri Lankans are, and make good speeches on every public occasion where they can grab some attention. The speeches are often replete with quotations from Buddhist scriptures and pieces of rhyming poetry that are made up spontaneously. Many of them preferred to wear the loose cotton white lungi and shirt, erroneously dubbed the national dress, to demonstrate their humility and fellowship with the poor, as opposed to those who wore European dress. But private insights revealed a different kind of people.

Our minister was in competition with at least two others for leadership of the country when the presidency should become vacant. Each had his own publicity machine directed both at the public and the MPs in the governing party. Departments and business corporations within their ministries, as well as ministry officials, were expected to support these aspirations. Each had his very own private national development fund: one for housing, another for education, and our minister for land allocation to low income farmers and a second one for the development of his electorate.

To be in close harmony with the local MPs and gain their loyalty, the minister held regular meetings with them, accompanied by his heads of departments in each province in rotation, to discuss local development issues. The local MPs, District Ministers and the most senior government officials in the area attended. The meetings were held in the provincial capital, usually in a hotel or government rest house, where the MPs were also lodged for the night at Ministry expense.

I declined to attend most of these provincial meetings on the grounds that I had urgent work and allowed the Working Director to represent the STC. The few I attended were very insightful. The MPs were usually concerned with what is referred to in America as *pork barrel* projects, promoting projects that delivered more goodies to their associates than to the electorate. But one incident that I witnessed shook my faith in the whole system that allowed some of these people to become partners in governing the country. At a meeting in the North Western Province, an MP noted for his rowdy behaviour, got up and started abusing the Government Agent, the head of the public service in the province, in the foulest language, using the epithet *pariah* on several occasions, for refusing to accede to his demands. The minister, who was presiding was embarrassed and sternly told him, 'Will the MP sit down at once'. But the man was not deterred. He continued his vulgar tirade till the minister called the other MPs to force him down to his chair. The poor Government Agent laid his head on the table and covered his ears and was silent throughout the rest of the meeting.

After such meetings, most MPs who retired for the night at the local rest house or hotel would keep the waiters busy with shouts of 'Bring another round of whisky!' They would gather in rooms and gossip about local politics and their deeds. Very often there would be references to some government official who would not accommodate their requests to appoint, transfer or promote some of their cronies. The usual conclusion was that such obstructionists should not be tolerated and should be harassed or removed from office.

Though ordinary people in the country tended to accept top politicians as feudal overlords, there were still hardy souls who thought otherwise. One day our Minister summoned me for a meeting and made a proposition: 'Kenneth, I discovered that there is a beautiful holiday bungalow in a hill station run by some foreign charity. It is managed by some old codger who was in the army. I am using my authority as Minister of Lands to acquire the property for a public purpose in the name of the State Timber Corporation. We can take it over and use it as a holiday bungalow for ourselves. I want you to have the notice of acquisition delivered and take over the building.'

'Who is this army chap who manages the place?' was my response. 'Let's see. Yes, the document says it is a Colonel Wickramasooriya.' Now Colonel Wickramasooriya was a retired army officer of the old school who had befriended me in my younger years. He would invite me to his residence for dinner whenever I was in Diyatalawa and his English wife was a charming hostess. The Colonel had had his higher education in England and belonged to a different cultural tradition. I told the minister, 'I am sorry Sir. I won't do it. The Colonel is a friend of mine.' 'Well, in that case I will get an officer from the ministry to do it.'

And that is when it happened. The ministry official went over to hand the Notice of Acquisition. The Colonel threw it back at the man and yelled: 'This institution belongs to the British government and is for retired British servicemen. Now get the hell out of here or I will get my shotgun to show you out.' The astonished officer fled and there the matter ended.

Sri Lanka, like many other democracies, basically has a two party system, with smaller extremist race-based parties playing the role of kingmaker. One or the other of these major parties will invariably govern the country.[6] But the drawback is that the parties are not democratic in their internal structure and this makes for governments that are less than democratic. In the USA, for example, the party nominees for political office are chosen on the basis of voting by party supporters, both by ballots in each State and, additionally, in the case of the presidency, by party caucuses. In Sri Lanka, as in the times of the ancient monarchies, powerful aristocratic families dominate the two parties which revolve round them. People tend to revere these aristocrats, as they revered the feudal overlords in the past. The party membership cannot dislodge these leading families. They nominate candidates for political office and the electorate then has little choice but to vote for one of them. The best potential candidates, who may be unwilling to be sycophants of the ruling families, will rarely gain nomination.

The public attitude to the political parties seemed to express their helplessness. When a party was in power, all government offices carried pictures of the president, prime minister and line minister

---

[6] An American scholar named Jane Russell analyzed this family domination of Sri Lankan politics in an excellent piece of research.

in the entrance hall. South Asians have a long tradition of hanging pictures of gods on their walls and these were the reigning gods. But thanks to universal adult franchise, granted by a British government in 1930, against the opposition of all leading politicians in Sri Lanka at the time except the communist leader, Dr S.A. Wickramasinghe, the governing power swings from one party to the other with regularity. When a government is defeated at the polls, the pictures of its leaders are torn from the walls of government offices, smashed underfoot and spat upon, and replaced by those of the victors. This is how the ordinary citizen can express his frustration.

21

IMAGE BUILDING

IMAGE BUILDING BY A BUSINESS IS NOT JUST A MATTER OF PUBLIC relations as a good public image influences employees and gives them a sense of the value of their work. It bolsters morale and imbues people with a pride in themselves.

When we came to the STC in early 1979, it was an obscure public sector business not very well known to the public at large despite having 2,100 employees. It gained some notoriety in Sri Lanka and abroad in environmental circles when it was employed by the government to log the pristine Sinharaja natural forest in Southern Sri Lanka, with its unique and still incompletely mapped flora and fauna, with assistance from the Canadian International Aid Agency, CIDA. Sinharaja was the last remnant of natural equatorial rain-forest that covered one third of the country till a hundred years or so ago. Two years later, based on election promises resulting from widespread condemnation of the project nationally and internation-ally, the new government cancelled this project. My friends had earlier expressed their concern that I was leaving an internationally known multinational corporation to join this obscure and troubled business. Yet within one year, the STC was a household name in Sri Lanka.

One of the first things I noticed, as an experienced marketing man, when I sat in my office at the STC, was how unsightly the office letterhead looked. Printed on poor quality paper and designed perhaps by a clerk in the office at one time, it looked horribly ugly. The STC logo was a crude outline of an elephant from the front but it was hard to identify due to the numerous lines in the drawing. I got down the international advertising agency, Thompson Associates, that I had worked with at XYZ Company and got them to redesign both the letterhead and logo and had new stationary printed using good quality paper.

The new logo was a stylized elephant head, based on an inspired moment that I had. The advertising agency did a good rendition of this. In future, all STC offices and work points would carry large name boards featuring this distinctive logo of the STC. The next step was to improve the appearance of the numerous STC offices which were scattered throughout the country, as befitted a forest based company. I had no intention of building fancy new offices at the time. The chairman's office that also housed the offices of the top managers was a large house in a residential area. Other offices were scattered in different buildings. What was needed was a little cleaning, polishing and gardening. Broken old furniture was disposed off and good quality furniture was brought in. Air-conditioners were installed. Tea is an indispensable part of office life in Sri Lanka and every organization has a tea room and tea-girls and boys to serve the staff with tea at regular intervals. Good quality china was introduced to replace the practice of serving tea in single cups.

A year later, when the STC provided all employees annually with two made-to-measure sets of safari suits for the men and saris for the women, with two pairs of shoes, it lifted the appearance of the offices and workplaces from that of a run of the mill government organization to become more like an international corporation. Clothes not only change a person's appearance, they tend to make a different kind of person.

My personal driver, Siriweera, was a very humble middle-aged man with a constantly apologetic smile on his lined face. He had worn a sarong all his life and had never worn shoes. He was always barefooted, like many Sri Lankan workers at the time. He was reluctant to wear a safari suit, which would make him look like a *mahattaya,* or a gentleman, in Sri Lankan parlance. I had to cajole him and he finally reluctantly acceded to my request that he should wear at least the safari coat as well as shoes during working hours. However, despite my best efforts, he refused to be a *mahattaya* and remained a humble man all his life.

The next step was to make the STC recognized nationally. Annual Reports of state enterprises are printed on cheap paper and are usually photo-copied or, even worse, cyclostyled. The overall appearance is as insipid as the contents. The 1979 STC Annual Report was designed and printed by the advertising agency with a modern design and format, with colour charts and graphs as illustrations, to announce that the STC had increased its turnover by 150 per cent and had registered a substantial profit. In the Chairman's Report, I analysed the national market for timber and timber products and outlined our vision for the future. We then sent copies of the report to all Members of Parliament, all Secretaries of Ministries, chambers of commerce and trade associations, embassies and newspapers.

We received wide publicity in the press for our achievements. In future, business correspondents from the national media would contact me every month for news as long as I was in office. I built a good working relationship with the media and the STC was often in the news in subsequent years. We kept up this style of business as long as I was in the STC but after a few years since my departure the STC returned to its government-inspired style of doing business.

The best propagandists for the image of a large and successful organization are the employees and consumers themselves. Employees who are happy in their work environment and are aware of the achievements of the company will boast about these to their friends and acquaintances. This word of mouth communication by employees is more credible than any media advertising. And the STC employees did a very good propaganda job for the corporation. Consumers were happy with the improved service and the more liberal availability of products. Product acceptance had never been a problem as the STC always offered the lowest prices in the market for their goods.

Sri Lankans, like most South Asians, have a genius for organizing extravagant ceremonials. Even a humble villager or an urban worker will not contemplate a family wedding or funeral without the participation of a few hundred people who are entertained to an elaborate lunch or dinner, followed by hours of speeches by elders and distinguished persons eulogizing the principal people. It is no matter that the costs of this extravagance will put the family into debt for many years.

The STC was no exception, except that it now had the resources and was not a debtor but a major creditor by now. Sri Lanka was a highly politicized society and will remain so for a long time more. It is impossible for business, private or public, to ignore the politicians and survive: that is the price of democracy as we know it. As even in the USA, all major private sector business houses in the country make secret donations to both the leading political parties. The STC could not escape unscathed since, unlike other state enterprises, it had decided to deny politicians access to manipulate management decisions for their private ends. The politicians needed to be humoured: they were won over by elaborate public ceremonies which gave them the opportunity to parade before the public and publicize themselves nationally. The press and TV were always present. In the eventuality, the STC also publicized itself nationally.

In the three year period of 1979 to 1981, the STC opened on an average 15 timber sales depots annually. Each opening involved an elaborate ceremonial. In the case of large depots in major urban areas, crowds of over ten thousand guests were in attendance. The distinguished visitors, comprising the Members of Parliament, Cabinet Ministers, District Ministers, even the Speaker of the House of Parliament, were brought to the stage in processions preceded by musicians and traditional dancers. Proceedings in the Sinhala Buddhist Southern Sri Lanka opened with invocations and ritual chants by Buddhist monks. In the Tamil Northern Sri Lanka the STC had Hindu religious rituals and Hindu priests blessed us with fire and ashes rubbed on our foreheads.

The Working Director and the Operations Managers displayed their inherited talent for organizing traditional Sri Lanka ceremonies of the elaborate kind. The stage for the speakers was surrounded by paper bunting and numerous flags. Temporary sheds with chairs were set up for the hundreds of invited guests while the thousands of other members of the public crowded into the open area around. The route to the stage was lined with palm fronds and flags and, sometimes, additionally, with overhead streamers of coloured paper. Loudspeakers blared out popular songs, disturbing the neighbourhood from early morning till the commencement of the ceremony, this being a form of public harassment that is tolerated in the country and accepted as normal behaviour.

Once the proceedings began, the traditional oil lamp was lighted and then speeches would go on for the next two hours. Sri Lankans are also patient listeners of long-winded politicians.

Since I had no expertise in organizing Sri Lankan tamashas, my role was to welcome the distinguished political guests as they alighted from their vehicles and preside at the meetings. The politicians and I were also garlanded on arrival by ladies from the STC. Sometimes, the task of garlanding our minister was assigned by the organizers to my wife. I suppose we all enjoyed the limelight.

22

SAVING THE FORESTS

TIMBER THIEVING IN THE FORESTS OF DEVELOPING COUNTRIES IS A worldwide problem. It is estimated that Sri Lanka has about 6,000 square miles of forest, almost all of it in government owned forests or forest reserves. Illicit logging in state forests is so rampant that the Forest Department and STC managers estimated that full one third of the timber for sale in the country came from illicit sources. About a third of the market was supplied by the STC while private gardens and estates, together with imports, supplied another one third. The law required that all timber logs transported on public roads must be accompanied by an official permit or should have the STC stamp on each log. The STC stamp is a designed indentation on the ends of logs made by a hammer and is used by STC supervisors to identify all logs felled by STC contractors at working points in the forest. Police and Forest Service officers are required to check trucks carrying timber to see whether they are authorized for transport with an official permit issued by the government or whether the logs bear the STC stamp.

In practice, as in many other parts of the world, timber thieves operate with impunity. They work with the patronage of local politicians and the police while other government officers are either coerced or bribed to tolerate the business. Illicit loggers were brazen enough to murder certain forest officers who had dared to check their activities. Since illicit loggers access timber without any payment to the owners of the forests, the government, the profits are high enough to be shared by many participants.

During this period, I made several press releases about the devastation of state forests by illicit loggers. This sometimes made headline news and there was pressure on the Minister of Lands and Land Development, whose ministry was responsible for state forests, to take action. The Minister summoned a meeting of the senior Forest Department and STC managers and spoke about the problem. He then announced that he was introducing regulations under the Forest Department Act to empower all STC managers also with the authority of the Police and Forest officers to apprehend illicit timber and seize the timber and the trucks used for transporting the timber.

The STC took the opportunity to create a Forest Security Department. Some of the senior operations managers were transferred to this department, making way for promotion of younger aspirants to their posts. I lost track of their work after a while but I knew that the Chief Operations Manager was monitoring the work of the Security Department.

After a while, it was reported that illicit fellers were very active in the forests around Mahiyangana, in the Eastern Province. It was very difficult to take action against these groups as they were working for the son of a senior cabinet minister, the MP for the area. Because this minister was so powerful, the police and forest officers were unwilling to interfere with their business.

I was summoned shortly after by our Minister. He said he was concerned by the news that the STC staff were colluding in the theft of timber by STC contractors working officially in the Mahiyangana forests. The news was given to him by no less a person than the MP for the area who was a senior cabinet minister. I told him that I was aware of the situation in the area but I could vouch that the STC employees in the area were not working with timber thieves. The minister seemed to be unconvinced. He told me that I should hire a helicopter and fly over the forest region so that I could see areas of denuded forest.

I did not take his request seriously. Denuded forests existed now because of the depredation the STC knew about. I informed the operations managers of the minister's complaint and left it at that. However, the STC managers, unknown to us, had devised their own strategy. About two weeks later, the Chief Operations Manager phoned me at night and informed me: 'Sir, we have used our authority and seized 14 trucks belonging to the son of the MP for Mahiyangana that were carrying stolen luxury timber. We apprehended these on the highway close to Moratuwa and have taken these to the police station there. They will now use their influence and get the trucks released. What can we do?'

I knew exactly what we should do. I had built up a good relationship with journalists from the main newspapers. I informed them that a big haul of illicit timber and the trucks transporting it had been seized and were impounded at a police station. The next day, reporters had gone to the police station, interviewed the police officers, and they published a front page news report of the timber haul, together with pictures. The names of the chief culprits were omitted.

As expected, the ministers used their influence and the trucks and timber were released. But the cat was out of the bag. The MP's son continued his illicit business till some time later when he was murdered by some rivals in the trade whom he had harassed to put them out of the business.

Similar episodes continued. On another occasion, the Chief Operations Manager again phoned me at night and told me of another interesting event: 'Sir, we have seized two trucks hauling illicit timber in the Mahaweli Area belonging to the brother-in-law of our Minister. We have impounded them. They will now come to you to get these released.'

'How is it that the Minister's brother-in-law is involved?'

'You may not know that his company has the contract to build luxury houses for expatriate managers in the Mahaweli Development Project. So instead of buying timber from legitimate sources, they found it convenient to steal from the nearby state forests.'

The Minister's brother-in-law was a powerful person. Most people would not have the temerity to get mixed up in his affairs. His company had expanded at a phenomenal rate with the number of foreign-funded government development projects it gained through his political connections and he was very wealthy. He had little time for people who stood in his way.

A short little while later I got another call, this time from the Additional Secretary to the ministry. 'Kenneth, a hell of a thing has happened. Your fellows have seized some trucks belonging to the minister's brother-in-law.'

'Really? Why on earth would they do a thing like that?'

'They were carrying some timber from the forest for some building work.'

'So why should that cause the STC managers to intervene?'

'The timber was not authorized. They had logged the forest on their own.'

'Oh! And so what do you want me to do?'

'Just tell your chaps to return the trucks and timber and let them off.'

I paused for a while and then spoke to him: 'You know, we were at the university together as friends and we had great visions of reforming this country at that time. Aren't you ashamed to make such a request of me?' He responded quietly, 'I am sorry, Kenneth.' But, as expected, the trucks and timber were released by the police the next day and the matter was hushed up.

Towards the end of 1979, I received a telephone call from the Minister of Transport. He spoke in a familiar way, though I had never met him. 'This is the Minister of Transport speaking. Is that the Chairman? Good. We are going to modernise our railways and will need a large quantity of railway sleepers:[1] in fact, we need about two hundred thousand a year. I understand that your corporation can't make these quantities. So we will have to look for other sources.'

---

[1] Railway sleepers are, in US parlance, railroad tiers.

'No Sir. That was in the past. We have just started clear felling in the vast Mahaweli Development Area. We are getting a lot of good hardwoods like *kumbuk* and *hora*, far in excess of normal market demand. I can assure we will give you the quantities of railway sleepers you want.'

'Well, we will have to see about that,' he said and ended the dialogue.

We hastily got together a meeting of the senior operations managers. The STC had produced and sold only two thousand railroad sleepers to the Railway Department in 1978. Could we increase this quantity? The managers agreed that the timber for vastly increased production was available. But the price paid to contractors to convert logs to railway sleepers was only Rs 50 and few people were interested in the business. Many of the *kumbuk* trees felled had to be sawn at site by the fellers because they were too large for the 10 or 15 ton trucks they used to haul logs. The procedure then was to dig a pit under the log and have two men sawing, using a long double handled saw, one standing in the pit and the other on the log. Once these were sawn to size, they had to be pressure treated at the STC treatment plants to withstand weathering to last for at least 25 years. The accountants worked out the figures and concluded that the STC could make a good profit even if it paid contractors up to Rs 200 per sleeper. It was decided to give the contractors this higher rate to build up large stocks.

Production of railroad sleepers then went up dramatically; from 2,000 in the previous year, 1978, to 14,400 in 1979, to 95,900 in 1980, to 147,800 in 1981.[2] Contractors were putting in new resources and working at high speed due to the attraction of the new rates from which they were making handsome profits. The Railway Department collection yards were getting filled up with little indication of the sleepers being used at the predicted rate of railroad renovation that had been told to us. By early 1980, a new constraint arose. The Railway Department said they wanted the sleepers on

[2] Figures from STC Annual Reports.

long term credit as they had no funds to pay the STC. The STC refused this request. The Railway Department did not make payments and the STC withheld deliveries and sleepers were now accumulating in STC yards. It was inconceivable that the Department would have started a major project without adequate funds from the government and/or funding by a foreign aid project.

In early 1980, I visited Thailand, Malaysia and Indonesia on a mission to see the timber sales and processing business in these countries which were major Asian timber exporters. In each of these countries, I visited the Sri Lankan embassy on a courtesy call. I learnt that some months earlier, the Railway Department had called for tenders in the three countries to supply 200,000 sleepers annually. The son of the Minister of Transport had then visited these embassies and personally interviewed the bidders. In Indonesia, I met the owner of one of the largest timber processing companies, Mrs Oudang, at a dinner party. She told me that the minister's son had interviewed all bidders at the embassy premises and wanted to know how much would be allocated as commission if they were to be given the contract. She said her company had withdrawn their bid in anger at the way he was bargaining for commission payments.

I came back to Sri Lanka and we found from Customs records that the Railway Department was paying about 25 per cent more than the STC price for imported sleepers. Also, it involved the loss of a scarce resource, foreign exchange. STC managers spoke with Railway officials and found that these imported sleepers were of inferior quality as they had not been adequately pressure treated.

This was a very grave loss to the country. The price being paid out to foreign contractors for 200,000 sleepers at US$27.50 each amounted to US$27.5 million over five years. I was incensed by this chicanery. I contacted our minister and asked him to intervene to stop imports since the STC product was cheaper and available. He replied that he could not offend another senior cabinet colleague by intervening in his work. I then wrote an official letter to the President of Sri Lanka, detailing everything that was happening. I never received a reply or even an acknowledgement. I then went to meet the Secretary of the Ministry of Transport. This gentleman was also a political appointee to the public service. He was a 'briefless lawyer', as they say in Sri Lanka, who was now prominent in social circles as he was a big spender at hotel dinner parties where he was lavishly using his official entertainment allowances that seemed unlimited. I had attended one of his dinner parties. He started off by ordering bottles of Royal Salute whisky, the most expensive brand available. Everything on the table was of the grandest sort.

I met him in his office. Good living had given him a corpulent girth and he had the half sleepy appearance of dissipated men who enjoy too much of the good life. We exchanged pleasantries and I then brought up the subject of imported railroad sleepers. I told him the STC was providing these at a lower price and that the railway department had stopped payments because the allocation of funds was being used for imports. He smiled lazily and told me bluntly: 'Kenneth, this Timber Corporation is not your own business. You make your money, we will make ours. Let's forget this subject. We will continue our work in our own way.' The matter was finished. The Railway Department did not pay the STC for the stocks provided and the imported sleepers were never fully used. A few years later, the Secretary died prematurely of a sudden illness.

The STC also made a contribution towards saving the forests. The Operations Managers, who were full of ideas for the development of the business, were keen on the STC establishing its own forest plantations. The Forest Department, which was mandated by the government to establish forest plantations and maintain all state forests, natural and planted, was not adequately funded to implement its tasks. Its annual budget allocation from the state was around Rs 40 million and most of this was used up by overheads. The royalty paid by the STC based on its sales revenues went direct to the Treasury, not to the Forest Department. The STC net profits in 1980, even after paying Rs 43.8 million as corporate taxes, was Rs 32.8 million.[3] After the cyclone of 1978 which levelled many

[3] Annual Report of the STC, 1981.

of the state forests in the Eastern Province, very little replanting had been done by the Forest Department to revive these plantations due to lack of funds. These had become barren lands and were being eroded by monsoon rains.

A proposal was prepared for investment in a plantation in a 1,660 acre section of the denuded land in Rugam in the Eastern Province as a pilot project in 1981. The plantation would be extended to 5,000 acres by 1982. The area was to be planted with mixed species of timber and medicinal plants, abandoning for the first time the monoculture that was the standard in traditional forestry. The proposal was discussed and passed at a board meeting, despite the opposition of the Conservator of Forests, who was a member. He requested that the money be allocated to the Forest Department for the work. But by now, flush with successes, the STC management was arrogant enough to believe that they were more efficient and productive than a government department with its archaic business practices, bureaucratic procedures and lethargy.

Large capital investment proposals had to be approved by the Ministry of Lands & Land Development, the supervising ministry. This proposal involved an investment of Rs 15 million and was sent to the Secretary of the Ministry. However, the STC managers were insistent that planting should start with the beginning of the rainy season and there was no time to lose. Several retired foresters of the Forest Department were recruited and put in charge of establishing plant nurseries. These nurseries were to be the most modern in the country as the STC was prepared to make investments in obtaining the best facilities.

The approval of the ministry was being delayed. After a few reminders to the Secretary, the STC received a very brief note that the forestry project was not approved. The Conservator of Forests had probably done his own lobbying against the project which intruded on his territory. The STC managers were in despair but I told them to go ahead with the work. I had other means of obtaining approval. The STC set a date for the ceremonial opening of the new plantation. Invitations for the opening ceremony were printed and invited the Minister of Lands & Land Development was invited to formally open the project. To encourage our minister, the STC invited all MPs and District Ministers in the Eastern Province to attend, invitations being personally delivered to them by STC managers. They were all assured of a large audience of local people to listen to the numerous speeches that such occasions demanded.

The minister arranged to hire a helicopter to take us to the site of the meeting and my wife and I were invited to join him. He was, as expected, happy that the work of his ministry was being publicised in this area of the Eastern Province, which was a Tamil speaking region, and that the local politicians would be there to see it. We had a very large gathering of about 10,000 people at the meeting area which was decorated with flags and had loudspeakers and a high platform for the distinguished people. Hindi film music was played till the meeting started. The audience had been obtained through the usual means: 40 trucks were deployed to transport poor villagers from the surrounding area, induced by the payment of Rs 10 plus a free lunch parcel for each participant.

Whether the Tamil speaking audience understood many of the long-winded speeches of mutual self-congratulation made mostly in the Sinhala language was not a problem. The meeting was a success and the project got off to a good start. We had by-passed the ministry officials and formal channels of communication. I found it necessary to act in this manner on several occasions if I was to get the work of the STC done. Innovative methods are demanded when the system is an obstruction to progress.

Saving the forests required extra conservation measures. Sri Lanka is a small country and its forest cover was dwindling annually due to the expansion of peasant cultivation as landless villagers kept encroaching into state forest lands. The extent of forest cover had declined to around 22 per cent of the land area and even here many of the forests were in a denuded state due to slash and burn cultivation and illicit logging. Some private traders had started importing building timber from Malaysia. This timber was of good quality hardwoods that had been well sawn and kiln seasoned.

But its popularity was limited. People still had a lot of faith in Sri Lanka's own hardwoods.

The STC decided to import some stocks of sawn timber from Malaysia. The sales performance of imported timber continued to be poor for a while. As a marketing person, I realized that we needed to promote the imported timber. The advertising agency was called in to develop an advertising campaign but we needed a brand name to advertise the timber. After considering many names that would suggest an association with the STC, we realized that one name would not work as there were at least two different species of timber that were being imported: *ballau* and *kempas*. Since Sri Lankan consumers were unaware of the names of these species, we decided to advertise *kempas*, a generic term, as a brand name. Kempas was the most popularly available Malaysian hardwood.

As a result of sustained advertising in the media by the STC, Kempas became a household word for a durable type of timber in Sri Lanka. It is very popular in Sri Lanka today and large quantities are imported by the private trade as building supervisors recommend Kempas wood to house builders. Hardly anyone is aware that the STC popularized this species of foreign timber which has saved so many Sri Lankan forests. But that is how it should be.

A little episode connected with this import is worth recollecting. I sent the General Manager to Malaysia and Singapore to evaluate the bidders for our tender for the import of timber. We could not evaluate the bids by sitting in a Colombo office as we knew very little of these businesses. We accepted the British company in Singapore he recommended. The company sent us a few shipments and we had good reason to be satisfied with the quality of the timber and the service.

The General Manager of the company, a Chinese gentleman, then visited us to promote sales. He wanted to have discussions with me and invited me for dinner with him at the Oberoi Hotel. I declined the invitation and proposed that he should be our guest for dinner in the same hotel. I made sure that all very senior managers of the STC, numbering about 15 persons, were participants at this dinner which was done in a lavish style. Our foreign guest sat next to me and kept whispering that he must have a private word with me. In the end, I acceded and went out of sight of the table with him. He promptly pulled a packet from his pocket and offered it to me. I told him that if he wanted to give anything, he must give it at the table to be opened in front of all the managers. He returned to the table and didn't mention the subject. I had to relate what had taken place to the managers after our guest had retired, to demonstrate the conduct we expected of our management.

23

MENDING THE SYSTEM

THERE IS NO LACK OF REFORMERS IN DEVELOPING COUNTRIES. IT IS just that they have more difficulty getting their voices heard. Several attempts have been made to improve public enterprise management in Sri Lanka and are, undoubtedly, still being made. We have referred to the short-lived effort of the Minister of Lands and Land Development and Mahaweli to introduce business planning and monthly performance evaluation in 1980. This was followed by the institution of a parliamentary committee, with the acronym COPE, to carry out a monthly monitoring of public enterprise performance. This was probably based on the recommendation of the dynamic Director of Public Enterprises in the Ministry of Finance, M. Somasunderam, who was responsible for much of the success it achieved at the time, not forgetting the MP for Wattala at the time who was its able chairman.

It must seem strange to us in developed countries that public institutions should be regularly monitored each month by a parliamentary committee consisting mainly of people with no experience of business and whose only interest is usually to make these institutions work for them personally in different ways. But authority in developing countries lies in the hands of politicians and this was well understood. The line ministry and the Ministry of Finance both have oversight of state institutions but public officials in these ministries would rarely intervene unless directed by the minister.

COPE did some good work at the time because the summarized monthly performance assessment of each institution provided by the Director of Public Enterprises, which provided the basis for discussion, was so incisive that COPE members were forced to focus on business issues, at least for a part of the time. Yet many members of the committee would focus on requesting an increase of work and employment by the organizations in their own electorates, without any business justification, and ignore the larger objectives of growth and profitability.

The scope of committees like COPE for improving the performance of public enterprises is limited. Politically appointed CEOs could ignore any strictures by such committees as long as they were backed by their supervising minister. The question remains whether there is any chance of improvement, considering that the politicization of public enterprises and institutions in developing countries cannot be eliminated. After many years of work as an international consultant on business development in developing countries and economies in transition, I am left with only two possibly workable proposals out of the many that I have recommended to different countries. We have to honestly acknowledge that politicians in power are not likely to give up too much of their acquired privileges.

The simpler of the two is the creation of a separate public enterprise management commission, consisting of senior retired professional managers (not public servants), who will supervise the development of business plans and carry out monthly performance evaluation reports to be submitted to the Minister in charge of the line ministry. This organization will also develop a database of qualified personnel with an experience of business from which public enterprise chairmen and directors will be selected. The minister will still retain the right to appoint his own people but they must be from this database of qualified personnel. The remuneration paid to chairmen and working directors will need to be substantially increased to make these positions attractive to qualified persons.

The other proposal is to give the management of poorly managed businesses on management contracts to qualified management firms. The methodology for this has been worked in detail in many development studies and does not need repetition here. Such management firms have not developed because of the unwillingness of governments to relinquish direct control of state enterprises. One successful example of this in Sri Lanka was the management contracts given at one time to foreign textile manufacturers to manage the government textile corporations that were in difficulty due to poor management.

On leaving the STC, I mooted this idea to both the Ministry of Plantation Industries in Sri Lanka, which had an ailing state enterprise that could have been turned around with improved management, and also to the two major development banks that were incurring losses through bad loans to poorly managed companies. There were no takers for the proposals. In the case of one particular proposal, our management company made detailed proposals to take over an ailing state enterprise of some importance to the economy. We wrote to the President of the country and he directed his minister to examine the proposal. Our detailed proposal and financial projections were examined by a group of senior public officials over several months, inconclusively. Then the final request came from a senior member of the governing political party through an emissary. He claimed that if he was made a partner in the project, he would ensure that the project was approved. The request was refused and the matter ended.

Politicians in developing countries are unwilling to believe that good management practices can make a difference to the economies of the countries. Two major privatization projects in Sri Lanka illustrate this. The bus transport services of the large Ceylon Transport Board were privatized and numerous small private companies and persons with no experience of management took over this fractured business. The result has been a chaotic transport network. In the other case, the nationalized plantation sector, that had declined over two decades because of state mismanagement, improved dramatically when it was taken over by a number of reputed business firms that had long experience in the business. As a result, tea production and exports have grown substantially.

24

A PARTING OF WAYS

> *. . . But in these cases*
> *We still have judgement here; that we but teach*
> *Bloody instructions, which, being taught, return*
> *To plague th'inventor: this even-handed justice*
> *Commends th'ingredients of our poison'd chalice*
> *To our own lips. . . .*

> —*Macbeth*, William Shakespeare, Scene VII.

THE AMBITIONS AND MACHINATIONS OF NATIONAL LEADERS unfortunately impact adversely on the lives of ordinary citizens. By 1981 it was evident that the octogenarian President of the country would retire from his position and three senior ministerial contenders were fighting undercover for the position. Imaginative but barely legitimate schemes were being developed to raise political funds for this purpose. Each of these contenders promoted his own development fund which also, incidentally, financed his political campaigns designed to win over party supporters and the government Members of Parliament. Life became difficult for public servants working in their ministries. Public officers were given targets to sell development lottery tickets that financed these development funds and business people and private citizens going to transact business in these ministries were obliged to buy these lottery tickets to get their business done, the bigger the business the larger the number of tickets to be purchased.

It was a period in the country's recent history when the legal restraints were stretched to the limit or ignored to accommodate state sponsored violence and, at the other end, terrorist violence against the state and its citizens erupted with a vengeance. Opposition to the government was met with severe reprisals. The Central Bank trade unions and the Nurses Union, among many, organized strikes that the government broke with extreme physical violence against the striking workers. A murderous pogrom against a minority community two years later left thousands of innocents dead. Terrorists retaliated by blowing up government facilities and killing thousands of ordinary citizens in their turn. Terrorist movements gained momentum both in the North and South of the island. Within the course of the next decade or so, the successful contender for the office of the President of Sri Lanka, as well as the two unsuccessful ones, had lost their lives to terrorist violence.

The story of the nurses' strike is worth recounting as I had it from the principal actress herself, whom I knew personally, as it typifies the politics of the time. The nurses union was on strike for better remuneration and working conditions. The government would not negotiate but sought to discredit the union through media propaganda, highlighting that it was unseemly that this essentially women's union was led by a Buddhist monk. The strike continued. According to my source, who was a government party activist and a former nurse herself, she was summoned by the President of the country and told: 'Girl, this is your job. Get these people.'

These people were got in the manner that was characteristic of the time. The activist went to the nurses living quarters housed in a large building complex and took position in the central quadrangle around which the buildings were laid. She screamed out to the inmates in their quarters, using the finest Billingsgate at her command. The nurses in turn came out to their balconies and shouted insults and jeered her. At some point, the activist sent a signal to the army of ruffians the state had assembled around the building complex. These thugs stormed in with iron bars and staves and rushed the nurses quarters, beating them up, tearing away the clothing of the screaming girls and smashing their possessions. After the mayhem was over, the strike was settled in favour of the government. This was not an isolated incident; it was in the character of the times.

I witnessed how the Central Bank strike was dealt with. Hundreds of Central Bank employees gathered for days in front of the bank building in the heart of Colombo's commercial centre, shouting slogans and waving placards. On this particular day, a line of buses drove slowly past the strikers. As each bus neared the first strikers, thugs armed with iron rods and bicycle chains jumped out to attack the strikers. They chased the striking employees and then boarded their bus which was slowly moving alongside them. Successive bus loads of ruffians attacked those who had come back or were straggling till nothing remained on the scene except discarded shoes and torn women's clothing.

A messenger from the ministry with an urgent message from the minister was announced while we were at a monthly management review meeting of the STC at the Taprobane Hotel in the latter part of 1981. A very ordinary looking character with a sly grin on his face walked slowly up to the head table in the meeting hall where the Working Director, Chief Accountant, Chief Operations Manager and I were seated and handed a sealed letter to Mr Wettewe, the Working Director. Mr Wettewe read it and turned ashen and his hand shook while he held it. He passed the letter to me without comment. The fellow, who clearly knew the contents as we understood from the bemused smirk on his face, waited for an acknowledgement and then left. It was a curt letter from the minister stating that Mr Wettewe was sacked from his position as Working Director of the STC with immediate effect.

I was as shocked and disturbed as the Working Director by this shabby treatment of a good man by the minister. I asked the Chief Operations Manager to chair the meeting and the two of us left for my office. The humiliation of this decent person in such a crude manner had obviously been hatched by the minister's rowdy cronies who were not able implement their plans for milking the STC because of his upright conduct. His pain also hurt me greatly. I told him I would meet the minister personally to demand an explanation.

I met the minister the next day but I was still in a gloomy mood. I had no more illusions about the man. His ambition was eclipsing the idealism he had in the past. I asked him why the Working Director was removed so summarily. His answer was shocking: 'Kenneth, you were appointed to manage the STC in your own way as a very good professional manager. That was fine. Wettewe, who is a relative of mine, was appointed as Working Director to look after my political interests. He has confused his role with yours. So I don't need him anymore.' This was the face of the real politician who often told me during arguments in private conversation that 'politics is the art of the possible'. I came away realizing that it was impossible to work with him much longer.

My relationship with the minister had developed to a point where I could not walk away from the STC without causing the displeasure of a powerful person and someone who had sincerely befriended me. But the excuse was not long in coming. A few weeks later, my family was invited to join his family for a weekend outing at a coconut estate in Chilaw, about 60 miles north of Colombo. After a few beers and lunch on that Saturday, I was invited into the office-room to talk business with him. He said he was aware that the STC was now an outstanding success story with large cash balances and he was very proud of it. That was excellent. He then made a request for a special favour that should be accommodated through the STC. It was an impossible demand. I refused the request in blunt terms, stating that 'Politicians may do such things, but I won't.' He was shamed and visibly upset by my sharp reaction. He called for an Air Force helicopter and left the location without speaking to anyone. The holiday party broke up and returned to Colombo, the others unaware of what happened except that there had been some disagreement that upset the Minister.

I have no doubt that the minister assumed that I would be grateful for being involved in his political ambitions. If he became the president of the country, I would also rise to high positions along with his train of loyal confidants and supporters. He had assumed that I would consider the highly immoral request an honour, as no doubt many others would have and as some of my successors at the STC did later. But I had told him that I was a reputed professional in the country and not a politician. He was confused by my reaction.

I assumed that our relations would be strained in future. But he was a cleverer man than I imagined at the time. I waited for a few weeks and sent in my letter of resignation to the minister, giving the reason that I planned to start my own management consultancy business. He phoned me and told me that he was not accepting my resignation, that he had put my letter in the waste-paper basket. He seemed to have forgotten the incident. But I had not. It would be impossible to continue with my planned work in the STC if I was not freed from the constant political interference that the minister was now using, contrary to the promises he made before I took this post.

A few weeks later the STC had the grand opening ceremony for its first forest plantation. The minister was the chief guest and he was very happy that the STC was organizing a large public meeting on the occasion and had invited all MPs and District Ministers in the Eastern Province to be present. He invited my wife and me to join him to get to the location and back by helicopter. While travelling, I told him that I would leave office at the end of the month in terms of my letter of resignation. He still refused to accept my resignation and told me that I could continue to do my own work and continue as Chairman of the STC, working part time. He laughed away my request as though it was a joke, saying, 'You could do your business while you are in the STC. You don't need to leave. Otherwise, I will have to make your wife the chairman and you can help her.'

In my last week in office, I sent a circular letter to all STC employees informing them that I would leave office in a few days and thanked them for their work and wished them well for the future.

The response to this was a stunning revelation of the great human qualities of the ordinary Sri Lankan worker. The STC Management Union came to me meet me within hours and on behalf of its membership begged me to withdraw my resignation. They said they could not contemplate the STC without my leadership. Then, representatives of all eight workers' trade unions and welfare associations came to see me. They represented the different major political groups in the country. They had gone to meet the minister and given him the petition copied below asking him to persuade me to withdraw my resignation. Perhaps they thought that I had been asked to leave for political reasons. The minister had replied that he tried to do his best to dissuade me from leaving but that I was adamant that I should now leave the STC.

State Timber Corporation
Colombo
28 October 1981

Hon. Minister of Lands & Land Development and
Mahaweli Development
Ministry of Lands & Land Development
Colombo 10

Request to defer the resignation of
Mr. K.L. Abeywickrama, Chairman, STC

Lt. Col. K.L. Abeywickrama,[1] Chairman, State Timber Corporation, by his message dated 23 October 1981 issued to the employees of the Corporation has stated that the letter of his resignation has been submitted to Your Honour for approval. All employees of the Corporation are deeply concerned over this unexpected news of his resignation.

[1] The Lieutenant Colonel rank comes from my having been an officer in the Volunteer Force of the Army.

All employees of this Corporation are aware of the benefits derived as a result of venturing into wide spread commercial activities under Your Honour's guidance by the present Chairman and Board of Directors appointed by Your Honour.

The employees who have undergone numerous hardships are now perturbed that the benefits achieved during the chairmanship of Mr Abeywickrama will be withdrawn. They are also worried about the future of the Corporation.

We would like to bring to Your Honours notice that all active organizations within the Corporation, in unison, have reviewed this unfortunate situation and unanimously decided to make the following request to Your Honour.

We all request Your Honour to use your good office to retain the services of Mr K.L. Abeywickrama, Chairman, State Timber Corporation, in order to obtain his expertise for the successful completion of the new ventures commenced by him.

Yours faithfully,

1. Jathika Sevaka Sangamaya (STC)
2. United Corporation and Mercantile Union (STC)
3. Sri Lanka Nidahas Welanda ha Karmika Ayathana Sevaka Sangamaya (STC)
4. Ceylon Mercantile Union (STC)
5. Corporation, Co-operative and Mercantile Employees Union (STC)
6. State Timber Corporation Mutual Benefit Association
7. State Timber Corporation Buddhist Association
8. State Timber Corporation Sports and Welfare Association

Copy to: Lt. Col. K.L. Abeywickrama
            Chairman, State Timber Corporation
            All Employees of the Corporation.

The tone of the petition directly addressed to me by the workers' unions and given to me at this meeting, it should be noted, lacked some of the obsequious references that are considered appropriate when addressing a top level politician in Sri Lanka. This is reproduced hereafter.

State Timber Corporation
Colombo
28 October 1981

Lt. Col. K.L. Abeywickrama
Chairman
State Timber Corporation

Dear Sir,

All employees of this Corporation have been informed by your message of 23 October 1981 that the Honourable Minister has been requested by you to accept your resignation as the Chairman of the Corporation.

This unexpected news has shattered all hopes and aspirations of the employees of this Corporation; employees are worried and uncertain of the future.

All employees gratefully accept the fact that this Corporation, activities of which was limited and concentrated in one direction only, has ventured into a wide commercial structure and created job opportunities to many.

All employees also accept the fact that the benefits enjoyed by them are numerous and comparatively much more beneficial.

We believe that you will accept the position that your devotion to duty and your experience in varied subjects especially of management and financial control are much more essential at this moment when you have just commenced a reafforestation programme for the benefit of the country at large.

All active organizations of this Corporation, on behalf of the rank and file of the employees and the country at large hereby earnestly request you to stay for a further period as the Chairman, in order to continue the good work you have been doing during the last 2½ years.

Yours faithfully,

1. Jathika Sevaka Sangamaya (STC)
2. United Corporation and Mercantile Union (STC)
3. Sri Lanka Nidahas Welada ha Karmika Ayathana Sevaka Sangamaya (STC)
4. Ceylon Mercantile Union (STC)
5. Corporation, Co-operative and Mercantile Employees Union (STC)

6. State Timber Corporation Mutual Benefit Association
7. State Timber Corporation Buddhist Association
8. State Timber Corporation Sports & Welfare Association.

Copy to: All Employees of the Corporation.

The top management cadre of the STC were more forthright in the expression of their fears for the future of the STC and their own future.

State Timber Corporation
Colombo
28 October 1981

Lt. Col. K.L. Abeywickrama
Chairman
State Timber Corporation

Dear Sir,

Employees of this Corporation have been informed by your message of 23 October 1981 that the Hon. Minister has been requested by you to accept your resignation as the Chairman of this Corporation.

   This unexpected news has shattered all hopes and aspirations of our employees; they are worried and uncertain of the future.

   State Timber Corporation established in 1968 was mainly concerned with felling and selling of timber. When you took over this sinking ship in 1979 we all met you and expressed our doubts about the future of the Corporation. As an experienced Captain you allayed our fears and we are proud to say that you have done the job successfully.

   You have introduced many management techniques. We are happy to say that most of our employees have responded to your call for good, honest and hard work. During your stewardship this Corporation has ventured into various commercial activities and made profits, beyond comparison to any other State Corporation. You have built such an image that we are proud to get up in any gathering and say that we are employees of the State Timber Corporation. We proudly say that 'Our Chairman is Lt. Col. K.L. Abeywickrama.'

You have just commenced a massive reafforestation programme for the benefit of the country at large. You have donated generously for other cultural and religious organizations. These are social responsibilities.

You have initiated action for the construction of an office building which this Corporation did not have for the last 12 years.

All these and may other activities commenced by you will not reach fruitful completion under any other mortal; this country has not produced many Abeywickramas.

On behalf of the entire rank and file of the employees who appreciate and value your good work and correct management innovations earnestly beg of you to stay for a further period as Chairman of this Corporation for the sake of your employees and the country at large.

For and on behalf of the Executives of the Corporation.

.... (12 signatories)

Copy to: Hon. Minister of Lands & Land Development and Mahaweli Development.

It was a stressful time for the STC employees and for me during this last week in office. Some of the female staff in the adjoining office wept as they came to plead with me not to leave the STC.

To all these representations, done in good faith and sincerity, I had one reply. I stated: 'We have, together, built up this business corporation and made it a success. The success of this is not the work of one person. It is a result of the management systems that we have jointly instituted and also the training of people and skills that the employees have so well demonstrated in their work. If this corporation has to depend on one person like me, then I would have failed in my work in the STC. If we have succeeded in establishing the correct foundation, the STC will continue to prosper with who-ever succeeds me.'

I would not change my mind. The executive staff, comprising about 75 officers, then planned a lavish farewell dinner for me and my family at a large hotel restaurant. Many emotional speeches were made praising me and I responded in kind. The senior staff had made a collection and they offered us a set of ebony chairs and an ebony table as a farewell gift.

25

EPILOGUE

THE PENSION PLAN FOR STC EMPLOYEES THAT WAS BEGUN IN 1981 was terminated by the management in 1991. The STC management of 1991 had decided that this was an unnecessary extravagance and terminated the plan and distributed the available funds to the employees. It was still a fairly large sum of money collected over 10 years on behalf of all employees. The contrast between employee and management relations in 1979/1981 and subsequent years no doubt inspired workers in the Colombo area to organize a token of appreciation of my work in an earlier era. A group of workers' representatives came to visit me after the pension fund had been distributed and said that STC workers in the Colombo region had donated Rs 100 each to conduct a Buddhist ceremony to confer merit on me.

I thanked them but refused the offer. They were adamant that they should do something on my behalf. I then suggested that they should give the collection to the inmates of the refugee camp situated a few miles from my house. These were needy persons who had lost their homes to terrorist violence in the Eastern Province some time earlier. They finally agreed and invited my wife and me to distribute the collection in the form of individual savings books to the camp inmates on a Saturday.

When we arrived at the camp we were greeted by a large gathering of several hundred people. A stage had been set up with microphones and loudspeakers and banners decorated the open ground where the presentations were to be held. The press and TV crews were present. There were many speeches by STC workers and management representatives eulogising me and expressing their gratitude for my past work before the handing of the savings books commenced.

All the major national newspapers carried a news item in the last week of August 1991, 10 years after I had left the STC and was planning to leave the country on a long term international consulting assignment, about a ceremony staged in appreciation of my services by the STC employees in Colombo. The text of the article and the picture that appeared in *The Island* newspaper of 21 August 1991, is in the Appendix. Similar articles with pictures appeared in the *Dinamina* of 21 August 1991, *The Daily News* of 23 August, *The Diva Ina* of 24 August, *The Lankadeepa* of 28 August, *The Sunday Times* of 01 September. The National TV, Rupavahini, carried a half hour film of the event the day after the occasion.

It was an emotional occasion for all of us. I was overwhelmed by the display of loyalty by these people, most of whom had not seen me for a decade. It had been my policy to avoid all official contact with the STC after I left the organization to avoid embarrassing the succeeding CEOs.

But other moves by the STC managements after my departure caused me some pain. The forestry training school we had established in Pimburettewe to train supervisors was closed down as a further sign of extravagance. Re-afforestation plans were abandoned, partly because of insurgent activity in the Eastern Province. The system of testing employees through written examinations prior to recruitment or promotions was abandoned. The STC became more politicized with the chairmen and directors spending considerable time on political work on behalf of the minister and accommodating requests from politicians. The STC sales turnover continued to grow, as I had predicted, to Rs 512 million by 1985 but began declining to Rs 395 million by 1986. Profits were eroded even further: in 1985 only Rs 26 million and in 1986 only Rs 18 million. These figures do not take into account the rapid depreciation of the Sri Lanka rupee between 1981 and 1985.

In retrospect, I realized that there were many changes to the STC which I had left undone. The STC had emerged from obscurity as a strong and viable Sri Lankan business. But the external world was rapidly changing and Sri Lanka lagged behind in relation to its South East Asian neighbours. The East Asian Tigers were rapidly industrializing and making their mark in world markets. Sri Lankan businesses needed to be integrated with the global markets to become strong players in future.

The 1980s saw the privatization of some large state enterprises in Sri Lanka, in accord with the growing trend in this direction in many developing countries. It was a beneficial trend on the whole, as it removed the avaricious grasp of the politicians from the management and the coffers of these enterprises. I had proposed to the Minister in conversation that some privatization could be introduced to the STC by creating a subsidiary for manufactured timber products which would allow a 50 per cent public shareholding, with 20 per cent being allocated as STC employee share options. This proposal did not find any favour.

However, all was not lost. In the next two decades, the private sector began expanding rapidly and with it the economy of the country. Many STC managers used the knowledge and the reputations they had acquired to move on to good jobs in large private companies. Others used the skills they had acquired to open their own business enterprises, often remaining in the timber business as importers and marketers. Imported timber became dominant in the market and the STC became just another player.

Almost everyone associated with the business, including many politicians, had seen that state enterprises could make effective businesses that served the state and the public. It pleased me to see in the parliamentary Hansard,[1] shortly after I left, that an opposition

---

[1] The official government publication containing the minutes of proceedings in the parliament.

Member of Parliament had questioned the Minister in the House on why the Chairman of the Timber Corporation, who he claimed was very efficient, had left the organization. The Minister had replied that it was a decision taken by that person which he could not change.

APPENDIX

Reproduced here is the article from *The Island* newspaper of 28 August 1991, about the ceremony staged by the employees of the State Timber Corporation in Colombo, in appreciation of my services.

STC employees salute former boss

About 300 employees of the State Timber Corporation (STC) who received a retirement benefit donated around Rs. 100 each and requested their former boss, Lt. Col. Kenneth Abeywickrama, to donate it to any cause of his choice. The presentation of savings books with these monies was made by the former Chairman of the corporation to the refugees in the Madiwala refugee camp on Friday, August 23 in the presence of a large gathering of corporation employees.

"In this world of changing loyalties and leaders, it is difficult to find groups of people who remember with gratitude and appreciation the work of former leaders and bosses. Old bosses are speedily forgotten when new stars appear. However, 300 employees of the State Timber Corporation reminded us that gratitude for past good deeds is still very much a part of our national culture," a corporation source said.

The State Timber Corporation, which was a small loss making business in 1978, was transformed under the leadership of Lt. Col. Abeywickrama into a large and profitable state sector enterprise during a brief two and a half year period in 1979/81. This transformation was the subject of a case study on effective management by the Harvard Business School, which is still used in Harvard, the Indian Institute of Management at Ahmedabad the Asian Institute of Management in Philippines and our own postgraduate institutes. The public at large may not have been aware that, apart from increasing sales and profits, he had developed a bond of unity between the workers and the management which the employees could not forget. So ten years after he retired from the post, the employees still wanted to make a gesture of their appreciation of a good job done well. (Pic. Sri Lal Gomes)

Kenneth Abeywickrama was born in Sri Lanka and graduated from the University of Ceylon in 1958 with a liberal arts degree. First employed for six years in the newly nationalized Port of Colombo as a Wharf Superintendent, he joined Lever Brothers (Ceylon) Ltd. [the largest consumer products company in the country], in 1965 as a Senior Manager in marketing where he later became Head of Marketing. He was sent by the company for management studies to Hindustan Lever Management School, Unilever Management School in UK and Ashridge Management College in UK. As the Export Manager, he travelled widely in the Middle East and Mauritius from 1973 to 1978. In 1979, with the creation of an open economy, he was made the Chairman/CEO of the State Timber Corporation by the new government which borrowed his services for a period from the company. The dramatic turnaround of this state enterprise became the subject of numerous management studies in the USA and elsewhere: a Harvard Business School case study (1981), articles in The *Asian Wall Street Journal* (22 and 28 September 1981), the California Management Review (Spring 1986) and in the book *Strategic Management in Developing Countries* by Prof. James Austin of Harvard University (Free Press of McMillan, 1990).

An active professional, he held elected office in the Committee of the Ceylon Chamber of Commerce for 10 years (1979–1988) and was Chairman of its Export Section (1978 and 1979), was a member of the Committee of the Federation of Chambers of

Commerce (1988), a member of the Ceylon Shippers' Council (1978–1982) and President of the Sri Lanka Institute of Marketing for two years (1977 and 1978).

Kenneth Abeywickrama was a prominent lecturer on marketing in Sri Lanka and lectured senior public enterprise managers in programs in Nigeria, Malaysia and the IIM in Ahmedabad, on behalf of the Commonwealth Secretariat.

From 1982 to 1991, he worked as a Marketing Consultant, working on long term assignments for 26 of the large cooperations in Sri Lanka. In 1991, he went abroad to work for the World Bank in Uganda and thereafter worked as an International Development Consultant, working mainly for the World Bank, UNIDO, USAID and ITC/UNTAD/WTO in Uganda, Kenya, Zambia, Lesotho, Sierra Leone, Sudan, Mongolia, Bosnia/Herzegovina, Albania, Sri Lanka and Austria, usually as the leader of multi-disciplinary teams. He moved to the USA in 1992 and became a US citizen.

The following are some of his professional publications: 'Upgrading & International Accreditation of Laboratories in Sri Lanka', published by the UNIDO/UNCTAD Cooperation Program for the project 'Integrating LDCs in Global Trade— Challenges and Opportunities of the Doha Development Agenda', August 2003; 'Factors in Preparing an Export Development Strategy for Albania', Economica of Albania, 16 May 2001; 'Post-Privatization Industrial Restructuring Issues in Transition Economies and Developing Countries', Tulane University Seminar Series, March 2001 (http://payson.tulane.edu/seminars/11-30-00.htm); Economic Change in Mongolia', Roundtable on Political & Economic Change in Mongolia, 27 March 1998; 'Privatization in Developing Countries', The New Vision, Uganda, 1993; 'Implementing Parastatal Reform: the Case of Uganda', Ministry of Finance, Uganda, 1992; 'The Case of the Ceylon Fisheries Corporation' and 'The State Timber Corporation of Sri Lanka', both presented at the Indian Institute of Management, Ahmedabad. He wrote six illustrated travel stories for the Ceylon Daily News, the Sri Lankan national daily paper.

HOW TO STOP SEXUAL HARASSMENT IN OUR SCHOOLS

DISCARD